Your Own, Your Very Own!

First published 1971

SBN 7110 0231 2

*Published by Ian Allan Ltd, Shepperton, Surrey and printed
in the United Kingdom by Ian Allan (Printing) Ltd.*

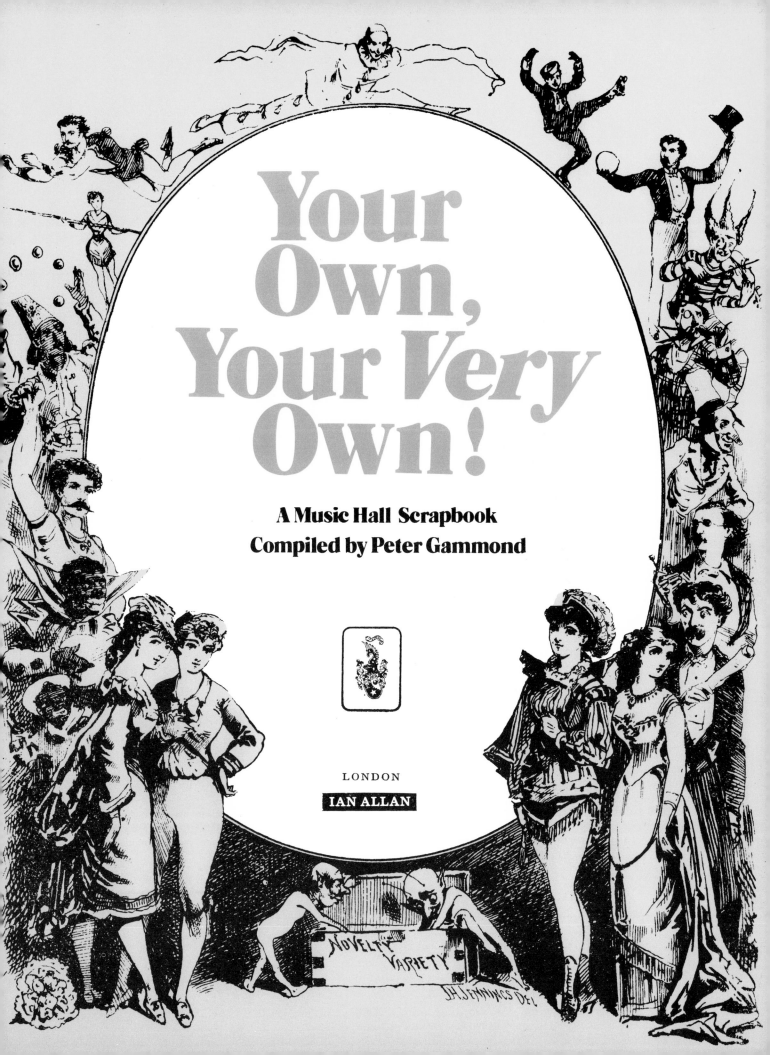

Your Own, Your Very Own!

A Music Hall Scrapbook
Compiled by Peter Gammond

LONDON
IAN ALLAN

12, St. Augustine's Road.
N.W.

Nov 22nd

Dear Sir,

I have no objection to your singing "He was a careful man", but shall feel obliged if (when you can) you will announce "by permission of the author" for I am determined to keep the song out of the Music Halls.

I am, Dear Sir,
Yours faithfully,
Geo: Grossmith Junr

W.G. Churchouse Esq

'In the better class establishments whole evenings pass without anything occurring on the stage to offend the delicacy of a lady; whilst, if we go lower, we shall find the penny gaffs, and public-house concerts, coarse, it may be, but on the whole moral, and contrasting most favourably with anything of the kind in France. It must be understood that I am alluding merely to the musical portion of these entertainments. Of late years the general increase of ballets and vulgar claptrap comic songs has not tended to elevate the tone of our music-halls.'

Rev. H. R. Hawes in 'Music and Morals' 1871

'Music-hall entertainment ought to be stupid, as surely as the drama ought to be intelligent . . . we did not come away wiser and better men; but an inward unity in the entertainment had formed for us a mood'.

Max Beerbohm in 'Around Theatres', 1903

'Even if theatres were smoked in and drunk in, they never would really rival the success of the Music Halls'.

Max Beerbohm in 'More Theatres', 1898-1903

'the very stuff of social history'

Rudyard Kipling

'I have no doubt the Academicals will turn up their noses at it. They don't like a tune that people can sing'

Arthur Sullivan

'Extraordinary how potent cheap music is'
Noel Coward

'The great virtue of the music-hall is that it jokes openly of those things which are commonly discussed in bar parlours'

James Agate

There have been many books about Music Hall and there will be many more, and my only excuse for adding one more to the list is that I, at least, never get tired of them. My own experiences of this kind of entertainment only extend back to seeing George Formby Jr., Will Fyffe, G. H. Elliott, Billy Merson, Harry Tate, Harry Lauder, Harry Champion and others in the days when music-hall had already become variety. We all have every opportunity to watch on TV some of those 'old-fashioned' comedians (young as well as old) who carry on the traditions, and we have seen the nostalgic revival of the song and supper style entertainment I often used to go to Collins Music Hall in Islington on a Saturday night and drank away my nostalgia in its picture-lined bar. . . .

So I, like many others, can only talk and write of Music Hall's heyday with second-hand knowledge; and yet I don't think that we feel at all out of touch with it. So strong is its aura, its legend, its tradition that we feel absolutely certain that we know exactly what it felt like to sit in the halls in the 1890s; our vision strengthened by the sight, feel and smell of old programmes, sheet-music, photographs, whatever remaining relics we can lay our hands on.

I don't claim to have a great deal more to reveal than others, closer to the real thing, have revealed already, but I hope I add my small quota of sidelights to the existing lore. I never get tired of probing into music-hall and trying to recapture its atmosphere, and I feel sure that an ever-growing band of enthusiasts feel exactly the same as I do. So I'll not apologise for this excursion; I am simply asking you to have a look at my own treasured scrapbook of bits and pieces and hoping you will enjoy the flavour of them with me.

My final effort is devoted to trying to document the field a little more thoroughly than it has been done before. Then you can delve on from my sketches into the wordy pages of those who were there. And if you haven't got the nostalgia disease already, I can only warn you that it is very virulent, very catching . . . and very enjoyable!

Shepperton 1971

Contents

Introduction

The history of Music Hall, and popular entertainment of the kind from which it developed, could be traced back (and probably will be one day) to various scratch entertainments in the courts of ancient Egypt – or even further. Picture an audience of paleolithic gentlemen, and the ladies they have dragged in with them, roaring with delight while the 'Great' Nog from Northumbria sings his latest success *It only hurts when I laugh*.

Throughout the pages of recorded musical history, which only covers a small part of all the events that actually happened (a particularly small part where truly popular music is concerned) we find evidence of people willing to pay a groat or two to be entertained by diverse singers, jugglers and dancers, with songs and side-splitting sketches. From patchy reports of such things going on in Elizabethan times, we move to more particularised accounts of entertainments at Bartholomew Fair. Then to the London pleasure gardens at Marylebone, Ranelagh and Vauxhall. Gradually, as our ancestors became less hardy and more addicted to the indoor life, to the assembly rooms of the Georgian taverns and coffee bars. Variously called glee clubs or harmonic societies, to hide their true bawdiness and conviviality, gatherings flourished in various pubs, with a noteworthy concentration round about the Strand in London, until in that same area (now sadly depleted of any signs of civilised life at all) there were developed rooms and cellars specially designed for the simultaneous enjoyment of food, drink and entertainment.

These Song and Supper Rooms, including the famous Evans's (late Joy's) at 43 King Street in Covent Garden (the façade still stands), the Coal Hole in the Strand, the Cyder Cellars in Maiden Lane – these all flourished in the early 1800s and provided a well fertilised seed bed for the growth of true music-hall. A great pretence to culture dominated them as demonstrated by the 44 pages of pirated knowledge and polite verse given away in the 'programme' to the customers at Evans's. But the level of the actual entertainment sunk to a much lower level than this pretentious literature indicated.

Before the coming of the music-hall there were theatres and halls offering light entertainment of incredible and vulgar variety as seen in the poster on page 8 . 'Come early!' it says on the bottom, a wise warning with so much to get through; but omits to mention what time it actually started – a trick that might well be adopted by the producers of well-meaning amateur theatricals. A great emphasis on 'dramatic' entertainment dominated these halls; while they exhibited a modest tendency to call their performers Mr. So-and-so, Mlle. Qu'avez-vous, and so on, christian names, as in the legitimate theatre, not yet bandied around with easy familiarity except in the case of a few of the leading actors.

GRANDTREAT

DON'T FORGET!

ROYAL

CITY OF LONDON

THEATRE.

FOR THE

BENEFIT

OF MESSRS.

CONY

AND

BLANCHARD

On Wednesday, Feb. 1, 1843.

TRAGEDY!

Melo-drama!

COMIC PANTOMIME!

COMBATS,

Dancing, Singing

&c. &c.

For this Night only, the Celebrated DOGS

HECTOR & BRUIN

The following Ladies and Gentlemen will appear on occasion—

Messrs. C. Dillon—Cowle—J. Dunn—Henry—Reynolds—T. Dunn—Brooks—Lloyd—Dove—Watson—Lambe—Manly—Smith—Sig Milano Mr. Atkinson—Signor Collinette—Mesdames Atkinson—Ellen Daly—Ridgway—Woolf—Johnson—Love Ward—Gay, and Mademoiselle Therese Cushnie.

DEMONIACAL DRAMA

FEATS OF STRENGTH!

The Performance to commence with the New Melo-drama by T. BLAKE, Esq. entitled The

BLOOD HOUNDS!

OR, THE

Orphan's Grave.

Master Mintlove, … Mr BROOKS, Joyce Gray … Mr DONE,
Master Oliver Howe, Mr REYNOLDS, Jaspard, Mr DUNN,
Stiletto, Mr LLOYD,
Master Hugh Lambert (the Solitary, a disbanded Lieut.) Mr DILLON
George Rippon (a young domestic, in love with Ady) Mr BLANCHARD
Dick of the Ferry (a Man of Desperate character) Mr CONY,
Job Snipe (surnamed the Witless,) Mr CARLES,
Master Pierce Gayton …..(a young Gallant) … Mr HENRY,
Master Adam Baxter … Mr MANLY Cavaliers, Troopers, &c.
The Bloodhounds, by Celebrated Dogs ….. } HECTOR and BRUIN
Ady Home, Mrs ATKINSON, Grace Robberds, Miss RIDGWAY
Madeline Lambert, Mrs COOKE, Herbert, an Orphan, Mast. CONY
Mabel … (the Goldsmith's Daughter) … Miss WOOLF.

OLD GOTHIC HALL.

The love tale—a Volunteer to the King—the Mariner's Fate—the abduction—the disguise—the moment of peril—the Night Brawlers

Desperate Encounter of Six

WITH SWORD & QUARTER STAFF.

The hired Assassin—Sagacity of the Bloodhounds—Narrow Escape of Dick of the Ferry.

Horrid MURDER!

WHITEFRIARS by Moonlight.

The Besiegers & the besieged—Rescue of Mabel by the City Watch

Burning of Baxter's House

Grand Fight and Sudden Appearance of

THE DOG AND DICK OF THE FERRY

Amidst THE BLAZING RUINS

The Old Gothic Hall.

The hue and cry—the lost Orphan—the price of crime—hopes & fears

The Murderer's Tale!

THE REPAST ON THE GRAVE

Sagacity of the Bloodhounds—Terror and Death of Hugh Lambert—the Assassin's Flight—Pursuit—Subterranean Vault.

The Denouement—struggle for Life

DESPERATE COMBAT!

FROM THE

WIZARD OF THE WAVE

By Messrs Cony and Blanchard.

The Murderer's DEATH

BY THE BLOODHOUNDS.

A Favorite Song,

By Mr. ATKINSON.

GRAND

PAS DE DEUX

By

SIGNOR MILANO,

And

Madslle. T. CUSHNIE.

SIGNOR

COLLINETTE

Will appear for this night only.

And perform several favourite TUNES on the

CASTANETS.

After which, the Demoniacal Drama of The

SKELETON HAND

OR, THE

DEMON STATUE.

Wolfgang …..(Leader of Banditti) … Mr COWLE
Herman Von Klishing, Mr REYNOLDS, Ludolph, Mr MANLY,
Stormo Von Rudeshum …… Mr BROOKS,
Hans Hoodekin, (fond of telling dreary legends) … Mr J. DUNN,
Dinny O'Loftus … Mr H. CARLES, Bruno, Mr DONE,
Scowl, …… Mr T. DUNN, Conrade, … Mr WATSON,
Demon Statue ……… Mr CONY,
Lestelle, Mrs ATKINSON, Barbara Schroolshausen, Miss DALY,
Banditti, Villagers, Soldiers, &c.

Leipsic Forest,--by Moonlight

Retreat of the Banditti—Seizure of Stormo Von Rudeshiem, by Wolfgang and his Band—Garden in Herman's house—Interview between Wolfgang and Lestelle—Herman jealous, vows to be revenged—Chamber in Herman's house—Dinny O'Loftus taken prisoner in mistake for Wolfgang—Garden by Moonlight—Pedestal with Statue.

TERRIFIC INCANTATION!

Herman endows the Statue with Reason.

Statue seizes Herman, and he becomes fixed as the Statue.

Mysterious Appearance

OF THE SKELETON HAND,

and Tableau—End of Act I.

ANNUAL BOOK FAIR

At Leipsic.

Ludolph denounces Wolfgang—Escape of Wolfgang and discharge of Musketry—A chamber in Herman's house.

Lestelle Terrified at the Statue

The Statue bending over her, protests his love for her—Robbers are about to carry her off, when the statue exclaims "Forbear" A dungeon—Dinney once more set at liberty—A Garden—Lestelle rushes in pursued by the statue, who still tells her that he loves her, and no one can save her; her father rushes in at the time, and is about to rescue her from the statue, when he

Seizes him by the Throat,

and lays him prostrate at his feet—Lestelle screams and faints! at that moment Wolfgang enters, sees her on the ground, and is about to lift her, when Ludolph enters in pursuit of him;

Ludolph sees his Friend Dead

and asks who has done this, when the statue exclaims "Behold the Murderer,"—A Chamber—Lestelle enters still pursued by the statue

She is about to Stab Herself

when statue interposes

Rocky Pass and Waterfall

Wolfgang led to Execution—Is about to be shot, when Hans Hoodekin enters, and satisfies Ludolph that the

STATUE IS THE MURDERER!

Statue seen on the point of the rock, bearing Lestelle in his arms when soldiers fire at him—Rock is blown up—Statue falls in the Waterfall—**LESTELLE IS SAVED**— Herman (when Statue is dead) staggers to front and dies—Wolfgang again saves Lestelle, and the

Skeleton Hand Appears.

Grand Tableau.

HORNPIPE

By Mr. T. DUNN.

CHINESE

DANCE,

By MASTER E. CONY.

To conclude with an entirely New Grand Supernatural, Classical, Comic Pantomime, with New and Splendid Scenery, Machinery, Dresses, and Appointments, entitled

HARLEQUIN

AND THE

ONE EYED BLACKSMITH,

OR,

The Genii

OF THE

VOLCANIC ISLE,

AND THE

Fiend of the Enchanted Forge.

Jupiter, alias Jove, { a whimsical Deity, rather inquisitive as to the opinion of Mortals } Mr. REYNOLDS
Vulcan { a well-known *Forger* (not of *Notes*) of Thunder-bolts, employed by his Father in manufacturing the same } Mr. ATKINSON,
afterwards **Harlequin** ……………… **Signor MILANO,**
Pluto, { a devil of a fellow for business, intimate with Vulcan, and on the look out for his *ashes*, alias Cinders } Mr. LLOYD,
Cyclops .. (excellent workmen, fond of their master, though much more susceptible of fear, with an eye to the forge) … Messrs. WELL EYE, CROOKED EYE BLINK EYE, and SQUINT EYE,
Neptune .. (Ruler of the Waves & Proprietor of New Warm Baths) Mr. DUNN,
Mercury, { an agile conveyancer of important news, with very little to say for himself, although of a hasty disposition } Mrs. DAVIS
Despair … (a melancholy fiend, attendant on Nox) afterwards
Pantaloon ……………… **Mr. CONY.**
Venus, { a beautiful Goddess, betrothed to Vulcan, willing to wed as soon as he returns } Miss WOOLF, afterwards
Columbine ……… …… **Mdlle THERESE CUSHNIE.**
Nox { a very *obnoxious* Fiend, a determined foe of Vulcan's with strong objections to Burning Mountains } Miss RIDGWAY
Discord .. (her daughter, a little like her, though not quite so ugly) afterwards
Clown … ……… **Mr. BLANCHARD.**
Lobsky & Lobscouse, (2 of the unboiled—not Policemen) Messrs. PLACE & SOLE,
Andrew McCraw { a full grown Crawfish, in love with *Lobscouse* trusting to come off with a *claw* "ECLAT," } Mr. LAMBE
Mats, ……………… ……… Mr. PRATE,
Finny Flanny … (a beautiful Maid (though not Liston's) .. Miss SCALES
Dolphins, Mermen, Crabfish, Flatfish, and others, by the Company.
Minerva, .. Miss LOVE, Proserpine, .. Miss JOHNSON,
Juno, .. Mrs. PEARSON, Leva, .. Miss GAY, Ceres, .. Miss GARDNER,
Goddess, .. Miss OFFORD, Diana, .. Miss HAWTHORN,
Flora, ……. Miss WARD, Hymen, ….. Miss PEARSON,

FIERY ABODE OF VULCAN

IN LAVA FURNACE OF MOUNT ETNA.

Where Vulcan forged the Bolts in Etna's burning glow—vindictive interference of an ob-nox-ious Fiend—mystic appearance of Father Jove's

CELESTIAL REGION

The Dwelling of the Gods.

The Complaint—The Petition—The Vote—gained by more hands than anticipated—Departure of the Celestials—Vulcan's Joy—the Fiend is Foiled.

Summit of Etna's Burning Crater by Moonlight!

The Watchful Fiend. The sleeping Hag. Flight of the Goddess of Sleep and Night, and her Sombre Abode.

Grand PANORAMIC Change to a Sicilian Landscape

Balae in the Distance—Romantic Pass—Fairy Lake, the retreat of Father Neptune.

Odd Fish—Queer Fish—Courtship of a Crab—a claw of its rival—an amorous Lobster—Water too hot for the unboiled.

ARRIVAL OF VENUS,

Accompanied by Neptune in his State (Sea) Carriage.

Real Sea Horses—Comfort of the Finny Tribe—Mustering of Deities—Magical appearance of the

VOLCANIC ISLAND,

IN FULL ERUPTION!

Mother Nox as obnoxious as ever—Queen of Darkness a foe to Light—Mercury's Mission ended—the Queen of Love—Venus the betrothed—Despair and Discord—To mar the peace of Jupiter's Forge—The Transformations—"commence the chase; yonder I take my seat, till those of mine are fairly beat,"—good friends at starting—Off we go by the Railroad of Fun!

REAL CHINA SHO

AND EXPORT MUFFIN DEPOT.

Mandarins in China, although in England—Harlequin Ferocity—Joints dressed and taken care of—Veal Pies—mutton, beef, kidne all hot—tureens and ladles—cooking on an improved scale—how dish up a lobster—lots of sauce—Clown dished—plates thos seasoned well—no Bankrupt, only made a smash—that's all.

HYDE PARK CORNER

Which of them?—Whichever you please my little dear.

Exterior of Chinese Exhibition

What! there you are again—Chinamen in England—national c osities—The Commissioner Lin, related to Lynn, of Norfolk—J Bull in a muddle—Joyful anticipations of cheap Indigo and Ch ney Ornaments—two tails of the Chinese—The Opium Questi

A CHINESE SETTLER—WAR JUNK—AN
A REGULAR MAN OF WAR,

The Treaty—21,000,000 Dollars at the cannon's mouth—don't wish I may get it, hem! Man-daring of Old England.

Corn Fields, 15 Mile from London.

Distant View of St. Paul's, London.

All on the Road to Scotland. Must go fashionable to meet Roya

EXTERIOR OF TOWN HALL, EDINBURGH!

Adjoining Sleeping Lodge. The Bailie's Residence. Preparati for meeting her Majesty the Queen and her Royal Consort.

Double Highland Fling

Mdle. CUSHNIE and Sig. MILANO.

Dancing Scotchmen—Fiddling Scotchmen—sleeping Scotchmen the Old Bailey and the New Bailey—Bag and other wind instr ments—Munificent Presentation of a

Real Scotch Fiddle, by Old Scratch

Good night old fellow—"all's well,"—not the Duet—Oh! M Bailie, unfortunate Mr. Bailie—you're Knighted, you're be-nighte—Harlequin invokes the aid of Somnus—Scotch fiddle dances; h doze-he-do. Transformations from

A regular Scotch M---l

LANDING of the QUEEN.

PROCESSION PASSING through the TOW

Bailie not up to snuff—pinch for time—fine Portraits of th Royal Visitors only—they are turned to the point of Danci mad—clocks wrong—your wrong—do'nt fall out—all th Characters compelled to join in a

GENUINE FLING FROM THE HOUSE.

A CELEBRATED

CIGAR AND SNUFF SHO

Not 110 Miles from the City Road.

Jim Crow in miniature—Grimstone's eye wide awake—Phr nology—and Plaster—Remarkable Heads of the People Punch and Judy—and the natural Organ—shew folly legiti mate, viz. Punch and his Spouse.

The Boundary Question!

Beaten by Charity Children—without the aid of Posts—out of th way—Punch bowled out—first appearance of the

London Chivarani in Comic Pantomime,

Pas de Trois, Clown, Pantaloon, and Punc

Broken Heads. Broken Images. Imagined ease. Mysterio loss of Gladiators. Re-appearance of some animation.

A Real Fighting Gladiator

On the "First Floor," supposed to be copied from a base relief in t

Glanum of the Ancients of Provenc

The

Mausolem of St. REM

But no such thing was taken from the Board of Images a few minute before—Clown statues—Ducrow's Music—played by Pantaloon—Clown proves himself a striking Actor—Old Lady and sever Gentlemen in a grand predicament—a Gent from Sham-bull-le supposed to be the Tobacconist, & by others to be his double Exterior of the Royal

City of London Theatre

Pilots ashore—Beadles abroad—Policemen at fault—unusual too-

A Celebrated Eating House

And Neighbouring Milk Palace

The Royal Exchange

In its Present State.

Covent Garden Marke

(Time) five o'clock in the Morning.

Fruit in Abundance. Lots for sale, but knocked down without bidding—who did it?—you—you—or you—my—a

Vegetable Turn-up!

Loss of Jove's Gift—Dismay of Harlequin—Clown's fancied suc cess—What?—Give him admission to the

VALLEY of VULCAN!

All matters arranged satisfactorily—Defeat of the Fiend—Welcom to the Enchanted

TEMPLE OF VESTA

Grand Tableau

AND FINALE!

TICKETS to be had of Mr. R. CRAGG, Royal Oak opposite the Pavilion, Whitechapel Road; of Mr BOXALL, next door to the City Theatre, and at th Theatre of Messrs. CONY and BLANCHARD.

Places may be secured at the Box Office.

Box 2s. Half-price 1s. Pit 1s. Gall. 6

COME EARLY!

J. W. PEEL, Printer, 74, New Cut

The final move toward the new music-hall came from the publicans who gradually found that a free helping of music and song in the right vein seemed to give people good appetites and thirsts. Such entertainment had long been provided at such places as the Eagle tavern (which people traditionally went 'in and out' of in *Pop goes the weasel*); and it began to have cumulative significance when several popular taverns on the South bank of the Thames began to open special rooms or saloons in order to cater for this perennial taste on a proper commercial basis. The Mogul saloon was opened in 1847; the Grapes in Southwark Bridge Road had its Grand Harmonic Hall added in 1848 – and soon took the historic step of calling itself the Surrey Music Hall; while Charles Morton, later to gain the honorary title of 'Father of the Halls', opened his famous Canterbury Hall soon after, having acquired the licence of the Canterbury Arms in 1849.

You obtained admittance to the Canterbury Hall (it didn't actually call itself the Canterbury Music Hall until after 1900) by buying a sixpenny refreshment ticket which gave you one free drink and as much entertainment as you could absorb. Contemporary reports speak of a well-lighted hall capable of seating some 1500 people. Morton kept his house on respectable lines and, after catering for the working-class only, such halls soon became fashionable and middle-class gentlemen began to take their wives and sweethearts along.

The further history of music-hall involves an incredible list of names and thirty or forty years of flourishing activity. Morton built his first famous Oxford Music Hall in 1861 (it was burnt down and rebuilt several times) by which period the following famous halls were already in existence:– The Mogul Saloon at 167 Drury Lane took on that name in 1847 and in 1851 was renamed the Middlesex Music Hall (by 1911 it was the New Middlesex Theatre of Varieties and became the Winter Garden Theatre in 1919, demolished in 1959 to make way for a new development which is to include a theatre); the South London Palace was built in 1860; the Bedford in Camden Town in 1861. Then came such famous halls as the Metropolitan in Edgware Road which opened in 1862 as Turnham's Grand Concert Hall on the site of an old inn dating back to 1524 which had a concert room added in 1836; it became the Metropolitan Music Hall in 1864 but has now vanished in the cause of ever-widening roads. Collins' in Islington was built in 1862; and so they came, thick and fast. By 1868 there were some 200 halls in London and its suburbs and some 300 in the rest of the British Isles – 500 variably flourishing establishments. No town of any size was without its music-hall (as later they were all to have their cinema). The bigger cities were only a step behind the London pubs in following the new pattern of entertainment; the Rodney in Birmingham, Youdon's Alexandra Hall in Sheffield, The Star in Bolton, the Parthenon Music Hall in Liverpool all started in the 1840s to be followed by the famous halls like the Argyle at Birkenhead which flourished for 72 years and was as much patronised by the big stars of music-hall, assured of capacity audiences, as any of the London palaces. But it becomes difficult to confine the list of memory-evoking names. A generation now in its mid-forties will be the last to remember sitting in the real musical-hall atmosphere; perhaps in a box at Collins' on a Saturday night, watching the peas shoot off the bald head of the musical director, and trying hard to enjoy the rather sad entertainment offered by those who had either remained faithful to the halls or couldn't get in on any of the more glamorous entertainment mediums.

The music hall era had a history of wild, reckless exploitation, as if it knew that its years were to be comparatively few. After the First World War the rival attractions of radio and the cinema began to lure away the audiences and to offer a more sophisticated kind of popular entertainment; undreamed-of rewards for the performers. TV probably came too late to be blamed for the final disappearance. Music hall had already declined into a glamourised version of itself called variety; which was to survive in a few London theatres merely to offer the chance of seeing a few TV stars in the flesh.

Interested parties are able to clearly pinpoint the first year of music-hall's downward path to 1914 when the LCC decided, in its wisdom, that drink and entertainment could not be allowed to flourish side by side and pushed all the drinkers out into those sad little, characterless bars which are now such a depressing part of our present-day theatrical tradition.

But we are concerned in this compact book with the great characters of music-hall – 'Your own, your very own'. It is not entirely true to suggest that names did not matter in the past; audiences have always flocked to see favourite dramatic stars, but the particular kind of star that the music-hall fostered was new. The music-hall was, in fact, the real start of a tradition that is still with us today as strong as ever – the singer and the song – the germ of all the frantic business that has been generated as 'pop' and has moved through many and varied manifestations. It will be noted on the front of Evans's hymn-sheet that a Mr. H. Clifton is mentioned in very small print; it was a very quick step indeed to the billing of **HARRY CLIFTON.** Again it was Mr. Morton who seems to bear a lot of the responsibility. Taking such men as Sam Cowell, Harry Clifton, W. G. Ross, Charles Sloman and Jack Sharp out of Evans's, the Coal Hole and the Cyder Cellar he gave them proper billing at the Canterbury and they got in the habit there and elsewhere of having their name in type three inches high. Mr. Morton also encouraged the habit of calling his stars 'the Great' this and that – the Great Vance, the Great MacDermott, and great is a word that has never been out of vogue since. So many show business personalities became 'great' that the word 'fantastic' has had to be introduced in recent years. From letters of three inches the variety stage proceeded to letters of three foot or more on the front of its various Palaces.

We have sketched in the geographical background to this cult of personality. Other factors also helped. The great improvement in transport meant that stars no longer loitered in their own provincial patch but more easily travelled the length of the country and went abroad to exhibit their glowing talents. The cheaper printing of music and its dissemination was another factor – we read on Mr. Cowell's poster on page 15 that *The ratcatcher's daughter* was already reaching the unprecedented sale of 228,000 copies. This was chicken feed to the million-selling that was to follow as the wildly over-productive days of Tin Pan Alley were set in motion; only to be cut short eventually by the wildly over-productive cult of the gramophone record.

If we delve into political and sociological reasons for the mad growth of music-hall during the late 1800s and the early 1900s we get into deep waters, but there seems to be plenty of evidence that it provided a vocal banner for the under-privileged section of our community just as it was beginning to get the idea that all human beings mattered even if they were not rich. This was the aspect that rightly appealed to the cultural gentlemen who began to write about music-hall in words of many syllables though, grant them, also in terms of true affection.

But it was mainly the beginning of the age of 'THE SONG' as sung by 'THE SINGER' and a tradition that now seems unlikely to die. We might take today, as a random sample, an excellent all-round entertainer like Mr. Val Doonican as a polished version of the type of entertainer who would have flourished in the music-hall. With a handful of songs made his 'very own' because he can sing them better than anyone else, the ability to woo an audience, tell a joke and join in a dramatic sketch – he is the 'compleat' and very skilled solo artist.

Before we delineate the quick profiles of our chosen music-hall stars, a brief word about the songs. Later in the book we have given a place amongst our chosen few to Joseph Tabrar, through fortuitious circumstances, as a typical music-hall composer. Such men would write a song especially for the star for a flat rate of a guinea or two – and that was the end of it as far as they were concerned. The song then became the property of the singer who made his fame and fortune out of it. Composers have come to their senses since then and are protected by the Performing Right Society and their various guilds and get a proper royalty; but the situation has not entirely changed. They may now eventually get a fat cheque instead of a gold sovereign but it still behoves a popular composer to writ for a very popular singer and it is still 'THE SONG' as recorded by 'THE SINGER'. It is only poetic justice to be able to point out that Mr. Irving Berlin is much better off and has more say than poor Mr. Tabrar whose death was almost un-noticed.

The music-hall artists chosen for our profiles are naturally those whose fame has survived even if only attached to one very well-known song. In time we end with Clarice Mayne who was born in 1891 and died in 1966. It is the birth date that is important. Being born on or before about 1885

which the room is devoted. A very few years ago it would have been possible to have alluded to this improvement at all; but to the present proprietor, Mr. Green, is due the honour of having elevated the moral tone of its amusements, and made them unobjectionable. This is no small honour, where profit was gained by the reverse nightly; and it required some moral courage to abandon the course altogether, as well as courage of another kind to hazard so much in the construction of this really beautiful room. It is a wholesome proof, however, of improved public taste, to find increased patronage rewarding both."—*Art Journal.*

A volume of very pleasant gossip might be written about the notabilities who have lived in Covent Garden within the last two centuries; indeed it has been a locality of great interest for six centuries past, or when it was the garden of the Abbey of St. Peter at Westminster—whence Convent, corrupted to Covent, Garden, which name occurs in the ninth year of the reign of Elizabeth. All our London antiquaries and topographers have found this "Garden" full of anecdotic sweets, which they have scarcely known how to leave, more especially as it has been for ages the great focus of town pleasure; and from its contiguity to the Cockpit and Drury-lane Theatre, it became early surrounded with taverns at which Clubs were held, and all the phases of gay life were recklessly indulged in. We must, however, beware of these attractions; for our present purpose merely to glance at the former fortunes of a small space, at the north-western angle of the Garden," before we describe the very elegant improvement which forms the subject of our Illustration. In this north-west angle, then, lived Sir Kenelm Digby, who was here much visited by the lovers of philosophy and mathematical learning. Aubery in his "Lives," thus distinctly points out the site of Digby's house.—

"Since the restoration of Charles II., he (Sir Kenelm Digby) lived in the last faire house westward in the north portico of Covent Garden, where my Lord Denzill Holles lived since. He had a laboratory there. I think he dyed in this house. Sed qu.'

The mansion was subsequently altered, if not rebuilt, by the Earl of Orford, better known by the name of Admiral Russell, who, in 1692, defeated Admiral de Tourville, near La Hogue, and ruined the French fleet. The house is built of fine brick; and, before recent alterations, the facade was thought to resemble the forecastle of a ship.

At the rear of the premises was a garden; and here was formerly a small cottage, in which the Kembles, when in the zenith of their fame at Covent-garden Theatre, occasionally took up their abode; here, we are informed, was the highly gifted Fanny Kemble. It is interesting to recall Sir Kenelm Digby and his grave friends, with their satirical doings and Digby's "Sympathetic Powder" fame, busying themselves in this identical garden, reduced in our time to a receptacle for a few sooty shrubs.

Meanwhile the great "singing-room" answered well its usual purposes until the character of the entertainment, by the introduction of music of a higher class than hitherto, brought so great an accession of visitors as to induce Mr. Green to extend his premises. He has accordingly built on the site of the garden (Digby's garden) an extremely handsome Hall, to which the former "singing room" forms a sort of vestibule. The latter is hung with a collection of portraits of celebrated actors and actresses, mostly of our own time, which Mr. Green has collected; and a more appropriate gallery he could not have assembled for the gratification of his visitors. The new Hall has been built from the designs of Mr. William Finch Hill, and is a meritorious work. The proportions of the room looking at it in section, is nearly square, being about 33 feet high, and as many wide: it is about 72 feet long from end to end; and with the old room, through which it is approached the Hall is 115 feet in length."—*Illustrated London News, Jan. 26, 1856.*

Amongst the eminent persons who resided here have been—Sir William Alexander, Earl of Stirling, the poet; he was living here, in the north-west angle, in 1637.—Thomas Killigrew, the wit; he was living in the north-west angle, between 1637 and 1643, and in 1660-1662.—Denzill Holles, in 1664, under the name of "Colonel Hollis;" and in 1666 and after, in a house on the site of Evans's Hotel, afterwards inhabited by Sir Harry Vane, the younger, (1647), and by Sir Kenelm Digby, (1652).

Digby spent the remainder of his life at his house in Covent-garden, where he was much visited by the lovers of philosophy and mathematical learning. At the breaking out of the first troubles, his library, which was justly considered a most valuable one, had been removed into France, and improved there at a very considerable expense; but, as he was not a subject of his Most Christian Majesty, the library became the property of the Crown, according to that branch of the prerogative which the French call 'Droit d'Aubain.'"—*Bio. Dic.*

The above-named Holles was a man of extraordinary courage, of which several in-

NEW MUSIC-ROOM COVENT-GARDEN

"Why do you not admire my daughter?" said the late Lady Archer to a nobleman. "Because," replied he "I am no judge of painting." "But surely," rejoined her ship, not in the least disconcerted by his reflection, "you never saw an angel that was painted?"—*Court Anecdotes.*

Andrew Lord Archer, married Sarah, the daughter of Mr. West, July, 1761.

Mr. West's library, sold in this house, occupied the auctioneer six weeks in the disposal of it. Books of the greatest literary value were sold for shillings. His MSS. are in the possession of the Marquis of Lansdowne. His books including many with important antiquarian notes by Bishop White Kennet, were sold by auction by Mr. Landford,—the catalogue ranged by Mr. Paterson. His prints and drawings were sold in thirteen days; coins and medals in seven. Mr. West was an early member and one of the vice-presidents of the Antiquarian Society; also, first treasurer and subsequently president of the Royal Society. The sale began March 29th. 1773.

In this house died Sir John Webb in 1797, leaving to his children (natural) the following handsome fortunes, to the eldest son, James, £13,000 a year, and £80,000 ready money; to John £6,000 a year and £100,000; to Fredrick £4,000 and £50,000; and to a daughter £2,000 and £20,000.

After the sale the house was used as an hotel, when the first family hotel in London was established in Covent-garden, in by a person of the name of David Low.

About 1790, Mrs. Hudson became proprietor. advertisements were numerous: one ends thus,—stabling for one hundred noblemen and horses.

Mr. Richardson succeeded the above. Joy followed; and then Mr. W. C. Evans, of Covent-garden Theatre, died in September, resigned it into the hands of the present proprietor in 1844.

Several actors have been inhabitants of this house. Amongst others, "the Knight," as he was familiarly called; and, during Mr. Charles Kemble's residence, it is asserted Mrs. Fanny Kemble was born in the room which forms the Gallery to the New Music Hall.

At the beginning of the present century, and for years afterwards, the singing-room was famed as a dinner and coffee room. It was called the "Star," from the number of men of rank who frequented it. One of the servants now living assured me "that it was no uncommon thing for nine dukes to dine here on one day. This was before the formation of clubs.

We may add to the memoranda concerning Evan's Hotel, that the Institute of British Architects held their meetings here when first established: here the first medal awarded by them was presented by the president, Earl de Grey to the successful candidate in 18—.

"Let us hie to the realms of Ap Thomas, to his warren of Welsh rabbits and his airy, spacious, cheerful, well-lighted halls, that he modestly names with the name of "Shades." We have not far to go. Only to the other side of the market—to the coyly retreating corner, where Ap Thomas and his social rabbits burrow underground. But though the entrance to the old haunt remains as in jovial days of yore, the interior has passed through many transitions until it is not the same interior but another. The hall of Ap Thomas could only pretend, at one time, to limited comfort; it is now a place of almost unlimited luxury. There are crystal "chandeliers," though the days of candles are numbered, and Ap Thomas, of course, burns gas. There is an army-corps of waiters, including a battalion of boys in buttons; and "attention" is more the order of the day than "stand at ease." In short, we have here the long-desired house of late entertainment, well-built, well-ventilated, well-conducted—off, dreary shameless brawler, of impure ditties, for Ap Thomas will abide no longer!—well-served and therefore well patronised.

We have just come in to hear "Blow, gentle Gales" and get a potato. Ah, here it comes. Fold a corner of the cloth round the tuber, and get gives a fair chance that the artiste (the final 'e' is important) would have been able to appear in real music-hall, before or during the 1914-18 war, rather than in 'variety' and the other deviants which followed. So we get a picture of what might be called the 'golden age' of music hall (although it was, in fact, the only age it ever had or is likely to have), from about 1850 to about 1915 – 65 glorious years.

The singers and the songs cannot, of course, be separated; jointly they survive, in the music – a couple of hundred of unforgettable songs remaining from amongst thousands already forgotten – in a handful of recordings and in the few pictures and programmes that survive. The architecture that surrounded them with plush and gilt has almost disappeared along with the social background that nourished them. The picture below of the Bedford in ruins after the blitz is a poignant memento of a great tradition – gone but not forgotten!

Acknowledgments

The credits for illustrative material, all from the author's own collection, are as follows:—

p 11   drawing from Evans's Music and Supper Rooms programme.

p 12   photo by Adam Woolfit and The Decca Record Co. Ltd.

p 14-15   details of cover, words and music from *The lost child*—Musical Treasury No. 779, Davidson.

p 16-17   details from covers of *Polly Perkins; Never look behind;* cover of *Percy St. Barbe* all Hopwood & Crew.

p 18-19   drawing 'The stage Irishman' by J. Bernard Partridge from *Stage-Land* by Jerome K. Jerome (Chatto & Windus); Lord Nelson Tavern from *Paul Pry* (1856); *The Irish wedding* cover—Musical Bouquet No. 2588—P. C. Sheard.

p 20-21   *Walking in the Zoo*—cover; *The idol of the day*—cover; and *Doing the Academy*—cover detail; all Hopwood & Crew.

p 22-3   details from The Empire programme 1888; cover of *Sister Mary walked like that*—Francis Bros. & Day.

p 24-5   cover of *Not for Joseph* quadrille; details from covers of *Et-cetera* and *The German band*—D'Alcorn & Co.; drawing by Maurice Greiffenhagen from *Footlights* 1895.

p 26-7   details of covers of *Love among the roses; Where is my Nancy*—Hopwood & Crew; *Captain Jinks* quadrille—Metzler & Co.

p 28-29   drawing of Evans's Supper rooms from Augustus Sala's *Twice round the Clock; Tommy make room for your Uncle*—Hopwood & Crew.

p 30-31   details from covers of *After the opera; Champagne Charlie; Night is the time; Under the sea*—Hopwood & Crew; words of *If ever I cease to love* by George Leybourne (Hopwood & Crew).

p 32-33   detail from the 'Harry Liston Songbook' —Chas. Sheard; details from *The rustic damsel*—John Blockley; advert from an Empire programme.

p 34-35   cover of *Says Aaron to Moses*—Hopwood & Crew; drawing of Morton by Tom Browne from 'The Days we Knew' (T. Werner Laurie); the Eagle Tavern from an old print; details from Evans's programme.

p 36-37   cover of *Co-operation*—Francis Bros. & Day; photos: H. Chance Newton (Elliott & Fry); Arthur Roberts (Raphael Tuck); (Rotary).

p 38-39   detail from Canterbury programme; cover of *The little vagabond boy*—Francis Bros. & Day; photos: Nelly Power and Jenny Hill (Sarony).

p 40-41   details from Euston Palace programme; details, cover and music from *Ask a p'liceman*—Francis, Day & Hunter.

p 42-43   cover of Oxford programme; details from Royal Canterbury programme; cover of *The blind boy*—Francis, Day & Hunter.

p 44-45   cover and intro music of *Two lovely black eyes*—Francis, Day & Hunter; photos: Charles Coborn 'The Man Who Broke the Bank'.

p 46-47   photos of Tabrar, Earle & Walker loaned by Mrs. Lily Walker.

p 48-49   cover of *Brighton*—Francis, Day & Hunter; drawing of Harry Randall by Alfred Bryan in 'Entr'acte & Limelight' 1887; of R. G. Knowles from 'Entr'acte'; detail from souvenir programme.

p 50-51   Pullan's poster; detail from Drury Lane 'Forty Thieves' poster; photos: Blampey Bros. & Rotary.

p 52-53   cover of *I may be crazy*—Francis, Day & Hunter; photo from 'Music Hall Pictorial' No. 3, 1905 (Denton & Co.); drawing from 'Entr'acte'.

p 54-55   cover of *'E can't take a roise out of Oi!*—Reynolds & Co.; detail from cover of *My old dutch*—Reynolds & Co.; photo: B. Knight.

p 56-57   cover of *Comrades*—Francis, Day & Hunter; detail from *Great White mother*—Francis, Day & Hunter.

p 58-59   details from covers of *It's a great big shame* (and musical introduction) and *Me and 'Er*—Francis, Day & Hunter; photo: unknown.

p 60-61   cover of *'Vesta Tilley's Popular Songs'*—Francis, Day & Hunter; photos: Rotary.

p 62-63   cover of *And other things . . .*—Hopwood & Crew; photos: Charles & Russell; Rotary.

p 64-65   cover of *Right on my doo-da*—B. Feldman; photos: Joan England; Music for Pleasure.

p 66-67   photos: cover of *Oliver Cromwell*—Hopwood & Crew; photos: Stage Photo and unknown.

p 68-69   Intro to *'Is pipe*—Reynolds & Co.; photos: Rotary.

p 70-71   cover of *Are we to part like this*—B. Feldman; photos: unknown.

p 72-73   cover of *A bit of a ruin* and music—B. Feldman; photos: Rotary and drawing from 'Entr'acte'.

p 74-5   cover and music from *Stop yer tickling, Jock*—Francis, Day & Hunter; photo: Rotary.

p 76-7   photos: Evening News; John Vickers (Ada Reeve) and Central Press.

p 78-9   Tivoli programme detail; drawing by Hassall; photo: Photlinol.

p 80-81   cover of *That's what he's done for me*—Francis, Day & Hunter; photos: Hana from 'Music Hall Pictorial' 1905; Music for Pleasure.

p 82-83   Pavilion, Glasgow programme; music from *Put me upon an island* and detail from *The Truth*—Francis, Day & Hunter.

p 84-5   detail from Holborn Empire programme; photo: unknown.

p 86-7   photos: unknown and S. Georges.

p 88-9   cover and music of *Jogging along behind the old grey mare*—Francis, Day & Hunter; photo: Sasha. dust-jacket: photos: Rotary; Ellis & Walery;

Covers of *Right on my doo-da; Are we to part like this; It's a bit of a ruin that Cromwell knocked about a bit* reproduced by kind permission of B. Feldman & Co. Ltd.

Covers of *Sister Mary walked like that; Co-operative; Little vagabond boy; Ask a p'liceman; The blind boy; Two lovely black eyes; Brighton; I may be crazy but I love you; Comrades; Great white mother; It's a great big shame; Me and 'er; Vesta Tilley's Popular Comic Songs; Stop yer tickling, Jock; That's what he's done for me; The truth; Jogging along behind the old grey mare;* details from above and musical quotations, reproduced by kind permission of Francis, Day & Hunter, Ltd. 138-140 Charing Cross Road, London, W.C.2

Covers of *'E can't take a roise out of Oi* and details from *My old Dutch* and *'Is pipe* reproduced by kind permission of K.P.M. Music Group (London) for Reynolds Music.

Covers and details from *Polly Perkins; Never look behind; Percy St. Barbe; Where is my Nancy; Love among the roses Tommy make room for your uncle; After the opera; Champagne Charlie; Night is the time; Under the sea; If ever I cease to love; Aaron said to Moses; And other things; Oliver Cromwell,* reproduced by kind permission of Ascherberg, Hopwood & Crew Ltd.

Drawing from 'Stage-Land' reproduced by kind permission of Chatto & Windus Ltd.

Every effort has been made to trace copyright owners of material used, but we apologise for any omissions in this respect.

Sam Cowell
1820–1864

Top: Drawing of Sam Cowell and details from the cover of *The Lost Child,* a song with words by the famous 'Punch' poet Thomas Hood.

Sam Cowell's is one of the earliest names to emerge as a music-hall star from that multifarious world of entertaining activities that added their ingredients to the music-hall proper. Such entertainers appeared in miscellaneous programmes that were almost circuses, they headed their own touring companies, they became well known in the song-and-supper rooms, and when the Canterbury became one of the first halls, they headed the bill there before the Leybournes and Vances had been built up into a new brand of music-hall artiste.

Others who made a reputation on the strength of one or two favourite songs that they introduced were John Moody – a celebrated mimic; W. G. Ross – who sang low class ditties like *The lively flea* and *Pat's leather breeches*, but was chiefly known for his macabre rendering of *Sam Hall;* Charles Sloman – who improvised rhymes on demand; Thomas Hudson with his *Jack Robinson* and *The spider and the fly;* and so on. But it was Sam Cowell who perhaps stands out as the music-halls' first great figure.

He was born on April 5, 1820 of Scottish parents, spending his youth in America where his father, an actor, was touring. They returned to Scotland and when Sam first appeared on the British stage on July 1, 1840 he was already a veteran whose first appearance in America had taken place when he was nine. He married in 1842 and a year later, with a son Joe, the family decided to take the plunge and come to London. Sam Cowell sung with an opera company at the Surrey Gardens, turned to comic songs at the Cremorne Pleasure Gardens and gradually relinquished dramatic acting to become a character singer in the song and supper rooms.

His success was largely due, as was the success of all the music-hall favourites who followed him, to his association with songs that caught the public's fancy and Sam Cowell had a particularly fine repertoire. His best number was *Vilikins and his Dinah* (which he took from Mr. Frederick Robson – a great character singer who had a considerable influence on Cowell – who first sung it in 'The Wandering Minstrel' produced in 1836). It fostered a long-lasting school of Cockney songs and comedians. He had comparable hits with *The ratcatcher's daughter; Billy Barlow* and *Lord Lovell.*

Cowell and his ilk were regarded as the 'fast' set; they added the spice that was much looked forward to in the otherwise staid entertainment provided. Much of the success of Evans's supper room is attributed to his pulling power. The chairman, Paddy Green, perhaps jealous of the comedian's popularity one day lost his temper, when Cowell overdid his habit of turning up late, and bellowed out: 'You've made Mr. Cowell your God, gentlemen, but by God, he shan't be mine!'

Many writers testify to his abilities: 'Sam Cowell was the best comic singer I ever heard' (Clement Scott); 'Cowell dressed his parts carefully . . . his favourite medium was a doggerell narrative running to many verses' (H. G. Hibbert); 'His artistic finish, incomparable style, and effervescent humour were not easily matched' (Stuart & Park).

At the Canterbury he rose to the unprecedented heights of earning £80 a week. Finally he set out on a tour of America, became ill and returned to London to die at the age of 44, his constitution weakened by too much good and hard living.

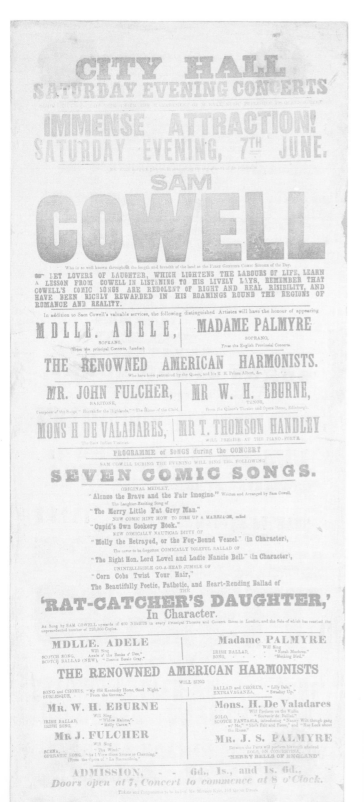

[Repeat from the 'Chant,' as in First Verse, to all the following Verses.]

Do, good people, move on; and don't be staring like a parcel of stupid young pigs
Saints forbid! perhaps he's been inveigled up a court, for the sake of his clothes, by the prigs;—
He'd got on nearly all his best, and they wasn't so very much tore;—
His jacket and breeches cost eighteen pence—but I shan't see him nor them any more.
Oh! will no one tell me where he's gone, &c.

He'd got on a very good pinafore, with two slits and a burn on the breast;
But his shirt, it's lucky I'd in the wash-tub, or it might have gone with the rest;
He'd a goodish sort of hat, if the crown was left in, and not so much jagged at the brim,
With one shoe off—and the shoe's a boot, and not a fit, and you'll know him by that, if it's him.
Oh! will no one tell me where he's gone, &c.

The last time as ever I seed him was with my own two blessed motherly eyes,
Sitting as good as goold in the gutter, a making of little dirt-pies;
Why should he leave the court where he was better off than all the other boys?
With two bricks, an old shoe, nine oyster-shells, and a dead kitten, by way of toys.
Oh! will no one tell me where he's gone, &c.

And, if I call him a beauty, it's no lie, but only as a mother ought to speak,—
I never set eyes on a handsomer face—only it ain't been wash'd for a week;
As for his hair, tho' it's red, it's the nicest red, when I've time just to show it the comb;—
I'll owe him five pounds, and a blessing besides, as will bring him safe and sound home.
Oh! will no one tell me where he's gone, &c.

He's blue eyes, and not to be call'd a squint, tho' a little cast he has got,
And his nose is still a good un, tho' the bridge is broken by falling over a pewter pint-pot;—
Oh, Billy, I'm as hoarse as a crow, thro' calling after you, you young sorrow!
And I shan't have half a voice left for crying 'red-herrings' to-morrow.
Oh! will no one tell me where he's gone, &c.

Harry Clifton
1824-1872

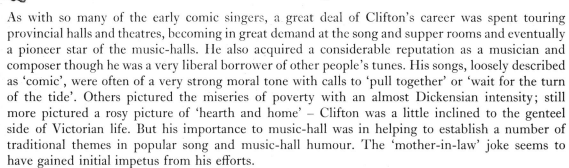

As with so many of the early comic singers, a great deal of Clifton's career was spent touring provincial halls and theatres, becoming in great demand at the song and supper rooms and eventually a pioneer star of the music-halls. He also acquired a considerable reputation as a musician and composer though he was a very liberal borrower of other people's tunes. His songs, loosely described as 'comic', were often of a very strong moral tone with calls to 'pull together' or 'wait for the turn of the tide'. Others pictured the miseries of poverty with an almost Dickensian intensity; still more pictured a rosy picture of 'hearth and home' – Clifton was a little inclined to the genteel side of Victorian life. But his importance to music-hall was in helping to establish a number of traditional themes in popular song and music-hall humour. The 'mother-in-law' joke seems to have gained initial impetus from his efforts.

Some of his songs are good enough to sound like folksongs and have earned their permanence in this light; especially *Polly Perkins* (which gains from a traditional air); but *Shelling green peas* and others deserve to be and will be better known as this field is more thoroughly explored. Typical Clifton 'uplift' ballads were *Paddle your own canoe* with the chorus:

> '*Then love your neighbour as yourself*
> *As the world you go travelling through,*
> *And never sit down with a tear or a frown,*
> *But paddle your own canoe.*'

Or, in *Wait for the turn of the tide*:

> '*Then try to be happy and gay, my boys,*
> *Remember the world is wide,*
> *And Rome wasn't built in a day, my boys,*
> *So wait for the turn of the tide*'

The *Sun* newspaper for July 8, 1867 had some warm-hearted words on the subject of 'The Songs of Mr. Harry Clifton' which are worth quoting:

'It is with much pleasure we have to speak of the humorous and pleasing compositions of this very clever vocalist and author, because they supply a want which has long existed, viz., a lively, merry ditty, that can be sung at a private family party, either by lady or gentleman, without the fear of offending propriety. Unfortunately of late a taste has to some extent sprung up for a class of songs of very questionable character and "great comic singers" have received in some instances enormous salaries for doing that which, in the opinion of many, had much better been left alone. But a change has begun to appear, and now real wit and humour seems to be required in place of low vulgarity. To Mr. Clifton is the favourable movement mainly to be attributed, because unaided he has worked against the vulgar taste . . . (*there follows a long list of his songs*) . . . in all such a healthy spirit prevails that the vocalist experiences as much pleasure in singing as a really merry and wise party would certainly feel in listening to them.'

Harry Clifton as portrayed on the cover of his famous song *Polly Perkins*.

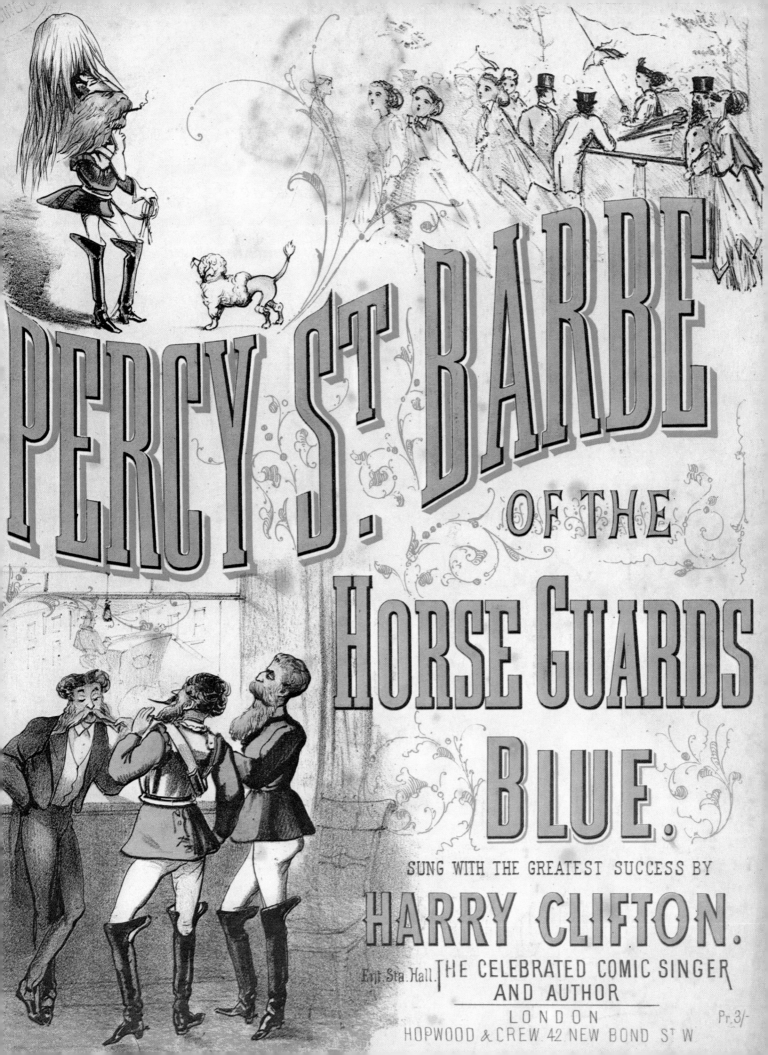

PERCY ST. BARBE

OF THE HORSE GUARDS BLUE.

SUNG WITH THE GREATEST SUCCESS BY

HARRY CLIFTON.

Ent. Sta. Hall. THE CELEBRATED COMIC SINGER
AND AUTHOR

LONDON   Pr. 3/-

HOPWOOD & CREW. 42 NEW BOND ST. W

Sam Collins
1827–1865

Another character well known at all the concert-rooms including Evans's was Sam Collins, whose real name was Vagg and who started out in life as a chimney-sweep. Amongst the spate of stage Cockneys he created another character, the stage Irishman 'from the caubeen on his head to the brogues on his feet, green coat of the pattern we call a dress coat now, drab cord breeches, worsted stockings and shillelagh'. He used to sing *The rocky road to Dublin* ('but we doubt if he ever trod it') and started his stage career at a fee of 7/6 a show and a hot drink. But as his fame grew he showed an unexpected Irish thriftiness and saved enough money to buy the Lansdowne Arms at Islington Green and to turn it into a music-hall which he was eventually able to sell for £50,000. Previously he had a business interest in the Marylebone Music Hall. Collins' remained a music-hall (with occasional sorties into the drama) until it was burnt down in 1958 and eventually demolished. By the end it was a somewhat tawdry variety theatre.

'With his jovial face and cheery manner' and 'a fund of genuine Hibernian drollery', he started his professional career at the Pantheon Music Hall in Oxford Street, but made his first great hit at the old Mogul (afterwards the Middlesex) in Drury Lane. Here it was his song *Paddy's wedding* that went down well, while his next successful number was *Limerick Races* which he sang with his usual 'quaint and humorous conception of character' at the Canterbury, Weston's, Wilton's, and other halls. Even off stage he remained in character, walking to his various engagements with his 'props' tied up in a cotton handkerchief at the end of a stout stick held over the shoulder.

Like so many of these early artistes, who lead a hard life and drank well when they had money – as a recompense for early poverty, Sam Collins died early, at only 39. He was buried in Kensal Cemetery with a handsome marble stone bearing his head carved around with hat, shillelagh and shamrock, and an epitaph written by his composer friend, Harry Sydney:

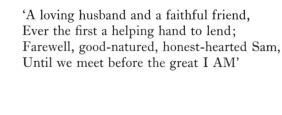

> 'A loving husband and a faithful friend,
> Ever the first a helping hand to lend;
> Farewell, good-natured, honest-hearted Sam,
> Until we meet before the great I AM'

POPULAR

COMIC SONGS

AS SUNG BY

THE LEADING VOCALISTS,

with

PIANO-FORTE ACCOMPANIMENTS.

THE IRISH WEDDING,

Sung by SAM COLLINS, &c.

WALKING IN THE ZOO.

SUNG WITH DISTINGUISHED APPLAUSE BY

THE GREAT VANCE.

ENT. STA. HALL,

Pr. 3/-

"WALKING IN THE ZOO, WALKING IN THE ZOO.
THE O.K. THING ON SUNDAY IS THE WALKING IN THE ZOO;
WALKING IN THE ZOO, WALKING IN THE ZOO
THE O.K. THING ON SUNDAY IS THE WALKING IN THE ZOO,"

WRITTEN BY

MUSIC BY

HUGH WILLOUGHBY SWENY ESQ. ALFRED LEE.

Alfred Vance
1838-1888

THE IDOL OF THE DAY.
PAR EXCELLENCE.

ALFRED LEE
THE GREAT VANCE

The rivalry between the two greatest 'lion-comiques', Alfred Vance and George Leybourne, was a perpetual source of interest in the 1870s and thereabouts. Possibly Leybourne won the battle by virtue of a stronger personality, more luck with songs, more vulgarity, to become *the* 'Lion Comique'; but Alfred Vance was always known (with the help of his agent) as 'The Great Vance' and well deserved his title. At one time the two comedians rivalled one another in drinking songs, at other times by seeing who could create the heaviest 'swell'.

Vance was a different type of man to Leybourne; quieter, not half so brash or blue in tone, subtler in his humour and depended more on his stage craft than on the flamboyant displays outside the theatre that the good-hearted Leybourne indulged in. Vance, in spite of his songs, was a moderate drinker (which Leybourne was not) and lived a balanced life. Even then, he died at 49, but where he would have wished to die – on the stage. It was on Boxing Day night in 1888 while performing, at The Sun in Knightsbridge, one of his moral or 'motto' songs. Dramatically declaiming the line 'Is he guilty?' he collapsed. The audience applauded a magnificent bit of acting but Vance was already dead as they carried him to the side of the stage.

Born, Alfred Peck Stevens, he was always a strong personality and soon rose to the top of his profession. Generally he appeared on the stage in a smart rigout of tight trousers, frock-coat and bowler hat, but he also had a great range of character parts. His songs, depending so much on his acting of them, have not been the kind to survive but they were immensely popular in their day when people could connect them with the singer more intimately. One of his greatest successes was *Walking in the zoo* – 'the proper game on Sunday, boys, is walking in the zoo' – which is not regularly heard now. Other hits were *Slap, bang* which had an inane refrain of 'ha-ha-has' and his great uplift song *Act on the square, boys*. Vance's gimmick was the friendly and continuous use of words like 'boys', 'my boys' and 'sir' with a sort of coy 'er' interpolated into his lines 'And – er – act on the square, boys, eh, act on the square' – touches which are not written into the songs so we have to imagine what a lot of sly meaning Vance put into them. His character songs included *Coster-monger Joe; Going to the Derby; The Chickaleary cove* – vivid portraits of Cockneys and, in the last named, of a dashing sort of crook. In between the songs Vance would interpolate a remarkable silent dance of the kind later to be known as the 'soft-shoe shuffle'. He was a great pioneering figure of the music-hall and many of the acts and actions that he originated are still with us – even if few remember the originator.

Jolly John Nash
1830–1901

THE EMPIRE
Theatre of Varieties.

John Nash was one of the first exponents of the 'laughing' song, hence the appelation of 'Jolly'. He made only a tentative start at the old Oxford in 1861, but thereafter soon became a very popular entertainer. The Oxford, the pride and joy of Mr. Charles Morton, was opened in March of that year with a high-class concert with singers such as the great Charles Santley in the programme – after that the Nashes took over.

Mr. Nash was one of the first music-hall stars to appear before Royalty and had the honour of performing before the Prince of Wales, on which occasion (partnered by Arthur Lloyd) he sang his celebrated song *Rackety Jack* and also *The merry toper* and *I'm not inquisitive*. The introduction to the 'Jolly Nash's Comic Song Book' says:

'Mr. J. Nash, familiarly known as "Jolly Nash" is generally appreciated as a Comic Singer of no mean order. He is, moreover, an excellent Musician and an able exponent of several Musical Instruments, among which the *Cornet* may be named, his performances on which have earned for him a considerable reputation.

For the last few years Mr. Nash has devoted his time to the Comic Muse and is universally known as the best interpreter of the "Jolly" class of Comic Songs – those that require a generous infusement of merriment, with a peculiar facial expression. Indeed, most of his songs are on the subject of laughter, with a laughing chorus; a cunning bachelor, a sly old maid, and a merry little fat man, are characters in which Mr. Nash particularly excels. His wonderful art of laughing, and making his audience laugh, is amazing; and it is no uncommon occurrence to see and hear some *Fifteen hundred people* joining him in a laughing chorus at the various Music Halls where his services are engaged'.

Elsewhere he has been described as 'a midland counties ironmaster whose jovial songs had been in great demand at Masonic gatherings' and had appeared, already quite well known in his teens, at various early halls. At one time, he returned to his iron business but, this failing, he came back to the stage in his thirties. His best-known song was *Sister Mary walks like this* which he demonstrated with an uproarious gait.

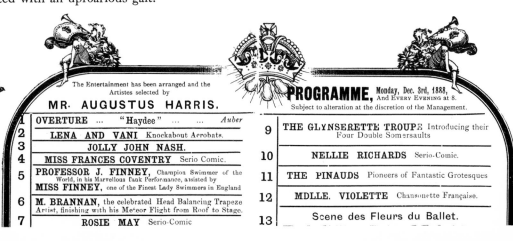

The Entertainment has been arranged and the Artistes selected by
MR. AUGUSTUS HARRIS.

PROGRAMME, Monday, Dec. 3rd, 1888, And Every Evening at 8.
Subject to alteration at the discretion of the Management.

1	OVERTURE ... "Haydee" ... ... Auber	9	THE GLYNSERETTE TROUPE Introducing their Four Double Somersaults
2	LENA AND VANI Knockabout Acrobats.		
3	JOLLY JOHN NASH.	10	NELLIE RICHARDS Serio-Comic.
4	MISS FRANCES COVENTRY Serio Comic.		
5	PROFESSOR J. FINNEY, Champion Swimmer of the World, in his Marvellous Tank Performance, assisted by MISS FINNEY, one of the Finest Lady Swimmers in England	11	THE PINAUDS Pioneers of Fantastic Grotesques
6	M. BRANNAN, the celebrated Head Balancing Trapeze Artist, finishing with his Meteor Flight from Roof to Stage.	12	MDLLE. VIOLETTE Chansonette Française.
7	ROSIE MAY Serio-Comic	13	Scene des Fleurs du Ballet.

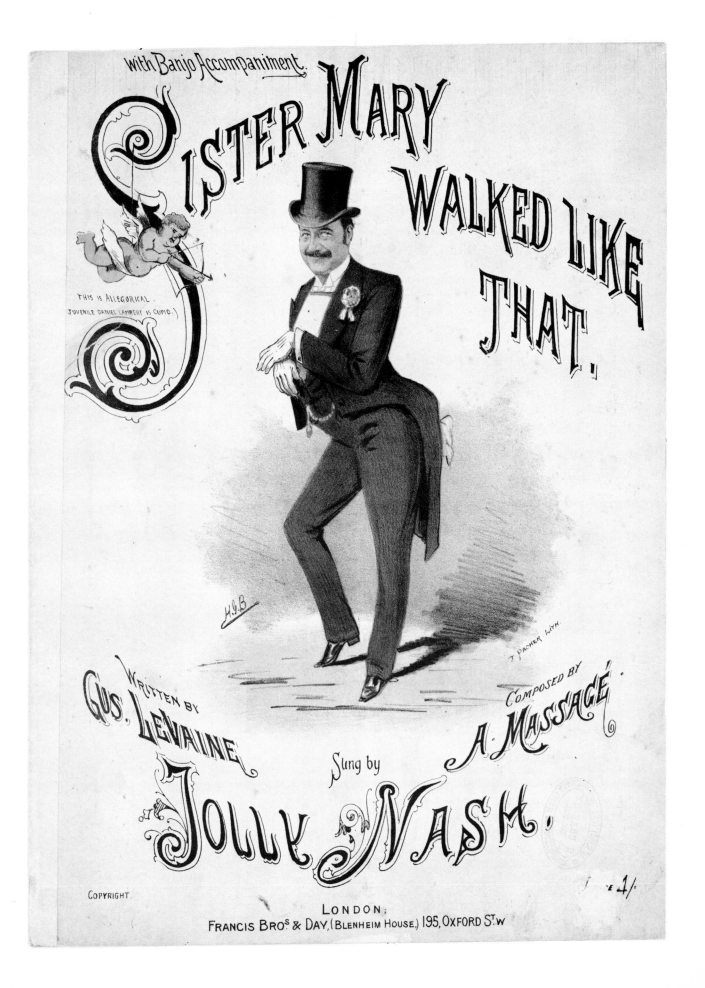

Arthur Lloyd
1839–1904

Drawing of the Music Hall 'Gallery' from *Footlights Annual* (1895).

Arthur Lloyd was a typical figure of the early days of music-hall, not just a star in his own narrow mode, but a writer, a producer and an impresario in a small way. Arthur Lloyd's Concert Party was a starting-off point for many names later to become well known. Eventually sharing the entertainment with 'Jolly' Nash in one of music-hall's first performances before Royalty – he made his first London appearance in 1862 after a thorough dramatic training in repertory. At the old London Pavilion he caused an immediate sensation – not so much as a comedian (which we somehow expect all music-hall artistes to be) but firstly as a fine singer, for he had a very good baritone voice; and secondly as a character actor – an accomplishment which, of course, helped him to put over his songs. Soon he was to be bracketted with Mackney and Sam Cowell, Vance and Leybourne, as a highly paid, much-in-demand artiste.

He certainly gathered a fascinating, varied and highly successful repertoire about him. His big hit was *Not for Joseph* which had a basically inane chorus which could be applied to anything:

> '*No, no, no, not for Joe, not for Joseph, not for Joseph,*
> *Oh, dear, no! oh, dear, no! Not for Joseph, not for Joe*'

and it was to be particularly applied to Mr. Joseph Chamberlain and became very much one of the 'catch' songs of the period. Arthur Lloyd wrote this masterpiece himself.

Another of his great hits was *Married to a mermaid* for which, it has been rumoured, no less a literary figure than W. M. Thackeray wrote the words after a convivial night at Evans's. Others in his book were *Take it Bob; The street musician; The organ grinder; I like to be a swell* (one of his roles was the 'heavy' swell, the lion comique of the Leybourne tradition); *Et-cetera* and *The German band* – a popular form of street entertainment in those days:

> '*They made an awful row, but still anyhow,*
> *They quite charmed the heart of Susannah:*
> *For she'd sit at the window, whilst the German flageolet*
> *Used to wink in a most improper manner.*

a bit of nonsense called *Immenskikoff;* and *Pretty lips.*

The final measure of Lloyd's success was perhaps that he died not too young and pretty well off, quite an achievement in those early and hard days.

"No dicky-bird singing up in the sky,
In the sky-was more happy than I,
But to happiness now I have said good bye,
For in pieces she's broken my heart."

Chorus. {
Does anyone know where my Nancy's gone?
Nancy's gone, Nancy's gone,
Does anyone know where my Nancy's gone,
Where oh! Where is my Nancy?"

SUNG WITH THE GREATEST SUCCESS BY

HARRY RICKARDS,

Harry Rickards
1842–1911

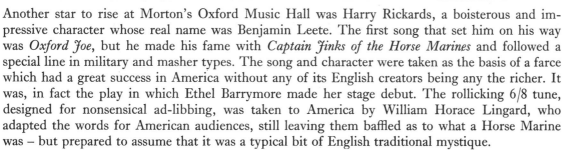

Another star to rise at Morton's Oxford Music Hall was Harry Rickards, a boisterous and impressive character whose real name was Benjamin Leete. The first song that set him on his way was *Oxford Joe*, but he made his fame with *Captain Jinks of the Horse Marines* and followed a special line in military and masher types. The song and character were taken as the basis of a farce which had a great success in America without any of its English creators being any the richer. It was, in fact the play in which Ethel Barrymore made her stage debut. The rollicking 6/8 tune, designed for nonsensical ad-libbing, was taken to America by William Horace Lingard, who adapted the words for American audiences, still leaving them baffled as to what a Horse Marine was – but prepared to assume that it was a typical bit of English traditional mystique.

Rickard did well enough for himself but, like so many of the music-hall singers, went in for management with his hard-earned cash – and became bankrupt. Eventually he went to Australia where he had much better luck. Soon he owned a chain of theatres over there, cashing in nicely on the spread of music-hall to 'down under' (they were always called 'variety' theatres in Australia) and quickly paid off all his English debts. No doubt, remembering his own struggles in England he gained a reputation as a generous employer and enticed many British artistes to his halls – including the Melbourne Opera House. When he died he left his family £60,000.

Not a particularly memorable artiste himself, Rickards was probably wise to get out of the struggle for recognition on the stage. We illustrate his song and a quadrille based on it as another interesting sidelight on Victorian musical activities. Most successful shows, operettas and the like, and many songs were purloined, not usually with any great financial gain for the originator, as material for the insatiable demand for dance music. The quadrille was introduced into England at Almack's famous dance saloon in 1816 and the English took it up with great fervour, until the polka became the next craze in the 1840s. A dance in five parts, each with its own steps, the first section being in 6/8; *Captain Jinks* was obvious material for adaptation.

W. B. Fair
1841–1909

Evans's song and supper room from *Twice Round the clock* (1860).

PERSONS of any age however bad their writing, may, in EIGHT LESSONS, acquire permanently an elegant and flowing style of PENMANSHIP, adapted either to professional pursuits or private correspondence. Arithmetic on a method requiring only one-third the time usually requisite. Bookkeeping, as practised in the Government, Banking, and Merchants' Offices; Shorthand, &c. For terms, &c., apply to MR. SMART, at the Institution, 5, Piccadilly East between the Haymarket and Regent Circus), removed from New-street, Covent Garden.

'Sung', as they said on the song sheet, 'with immense success' by W. B. Fair, it was the one great hit of this man about music-hall; *Tommy make room for your uncle* – confirmation of the value of a good 'catch-phrase', for there is little of musical or literary merit in the song itself. But its vogue truly was 'immense', so great indeed that it kept him going as an artiste for over 10 years, and he sung it at all the halls including his favourite haunt, the Rosherville at Gravesend. Some evenings he would sing it at least six times in different halls and it made him enough money for him to buy the Winchester Music Hall in Southwark Bridge Road (known locally as The Grapes). Previously he had been Chairman at the Marylebone, the Standard (where he was also manager) and the Royal, Holborn, but now he could preside in his own hall and give them *Tommy make room for your uncle* into the bargain.

Another sideline was a theatrical agency in the Waterloo Road in partnership with G. H. MacDermott, but Mr. Fair was no business man (perhaps he lived up to his name too well) and he lost all his hard won cash and ended his days as doorman at the London Coliseum – the common disease of over-enthusiastic drinking a contributory cause of his downfall. Immortality is ensured, however, for the song and its singer by a laboured reference in the works of Mr. Robert Browning: –

'Troop! all of you Man or homunculus!
Who, treading down, rose and ranunculus,
All Tommy Make Room for your Uncle'us.

Which is perhaps even greater nonsense than the song itself.

TOMMY MAKE ROOM FOR YOUR UNCLE.

WRITTEN & COMPOSED BY

T. S. LONSDALE,

SUNG WITH IMMENSE SUCCESS

BY

W. B. FAIR.

Price 3/-

George Leybourne
1842-1884

Details from *After the Opera, Champagne Charlie, Night is the time to have a spree my boys* and *Under the sea*.

Leybourne was the leading 'lion-comique' (a title invented by a well-known manager and chairman J. J. Poole) of the 70s and 80s; closely rivalled by Vance, MacDermott and others. Starting out as a labourer at a marine engineers in Westminster Bridge Road he soon decided to cash in on his handsome appearance and splendid baritone voice. He was probably one of the tallest and most impressive men to appear on the music-hall stage where talent generally comes in small sizes. The curious conflicts in Leybourne's nature seem to have fascinated most people. Although posing as the well-to-do man-about-town, the 'swell', he remained rather illiterate and often lapsed into the rough speech of his labouring days. On the other hand he would often enrapture his audience by relinquishing his comic masher songs to break into a beautifully sung 'straight' song or ballad.

It was as *Champagne Charlie* that he became best-known, often publicising the character by buying champagne for the audience. Unfortunately he was also living up to it in private life by consuming large quantities of the beverage he glorified. A short life and a gay one! When he first came to the Canterbury he was paid £30 a week (quite a record salary then) on the condition that he drove to his engagements in a brougham drawn by four white horses. He remained top of the bill at the Canterbury and the Oxford for some 20 years until he was earning £120 a week; a glorious rise from the young man, then known as Joseph Saunders, who first trod the boards in Gilbert's Music Hall in Whitechapel singing *The dark girl dressed in blue* for a few shillings.

He was a versatile artiste and truly one of the great actors of music-hall. As well as boosting the properties of champagne he had songs about Burgundy and Moselle and an item called *My name it is John Barleycorn* dedicated to the Licensed Victuallers Association. Food was also represented in songs like *The little eel pie shop* (in fact a rather quaint love song); while his range of characterisations ran from *Up in a balloon*, via *The mousetrap man*, to an evening *At the opera*. Some of his songs like *If I ever cease to love* and *They all do it* were very near the accepted limits of suggestiveness and Leybourne was warned by the law on one or two occasions.

He was a great man, adored by the ladies; as he sang in one of his gentler songs:

> 'Oh! she danced like a fairy and sang like a bird,
> She did, on my word, though rather absurd.
> But she fancied George Leybourne, a singer you've heard –
> And with him she skedaddled away!'

and admired by the gentlemen. A generous man with his money and always ready to stand a drink; in the end it killed him and his final years of his short life were a sad tale of rapid decline.

IF EVER I CEASE TO LOVE

WRITTEN, COMPOSED & SUNG
BY
GEORGE LEYBOURNE.

1

In a house, in a square, in a quadrant,
In a street, in a lane, in a road;
Turn to the left, on the right hand
You see there my true love's abode.
I go there a courting and cooing,
To my love, like a dove,
And swearing on my bended knee.
If ever I cease to love.
May sheeps heads grow on apple trees,
If ever I cease to love,
CHORUS. If ever I cease to love,
If ever I cease to love,
May the moon be turn'd into green cheese
If ever I cease to love.

2

She can sing, she can play the piano,
She can jump, she can dance, she can run,
In fact she's a modern Taglioni,
And Sims Reeves rolled into one.
And who would not love such a beauty,
Like an Angel dropped from above,
May I be stung to death with flies,
If ever I cease to love.
May I be stung to death with flies,
If ever I cease to love.
CHORUS. If ever I cease to love,
If ever I cease to love,
May little dogs wag their tails in front,
If ever I cease to love.

3

For all the money that's in the Bank,
For the title of a Lord or a Duke,
I wouldn't exchange the girl I love,
There's bliss in every look:
To see her dance the Polka
I could faint with radiant love,
May the Monument a hornpipe dance
If ever I cease to love.
May we never have to pay the Income Tax.
If ever I cease to love.
CHORUS. If ever I cease to love,
If ever I cease to love,
May we all turn into cats and dogs,
If ever I cease to love.

4

May all the seas turn into ink,
May negroes all turn white,
May the Queen in Buckingham Palace live,
May wrong be turned to right,
May cows lay eggs, may fowls yield milk,
May the hawk become a dove,
May Bobbies refuse to eat cold meat,
If ever I cease to love.
May I be frozen to death with heat,
If ever I cease to love,
CHORUS. If ever I cease to love,
If ever I cease to love,
May a sane man adore his Mother-in-law,
If ever I cease to love

Harry Liston
1843–1929

SUNG BY

HARRY LISTON,

IN HIS POPULAR ENTERTAINMENT "MERRY MOMENTS."

AUTHOR OF

FANCY GOES A VERY LONG WAY	4/-	GRANDFATHER SHOREHAM	4/-
HE'S WORSE THAN MY BIG BROTHER	4/-	MERRY MOMENTS	4/-
DID YOU KNOW MR SMIT	4/-	ANY VINDERS TO MEND	4/-

LONDON: JOHN BLOCKLEY, 3, ARGYLL ST REGENT ST W.

A lesser lion appeared in the shape of Harry Liston who cashed in on Leybourne's foibles from time to time and even arrived at the theatre one day in a small carriage drawn by four white donkeys. He was a likeable young man, a sort of Fred Astaire of the period, with top hat, white tie and tails, as it said in the introduction to Harry Liston's 'New Comic Song Book': –

'Mr. HARRY LISTON has sung at most of the London Music Halls, and is consequently well known and deservedly popular. In the Provinces also he is fully appreciated, and enjoys a high reputation. The Comic Songs of this "Pet of the Public" are so comprehensive in their character that his *repertoire* may be said to embrace every variety – the Drawing-room Comic, the Serio-comic, the Grave, the Gay, and the Low Comedy Songs. With an excellent voice, and certainly by far the most elegant and graceful dancer among Comic Singers, he is able to give due effect to his songs, and, as is now so much the fashion, to perform a dance or jig after each verse. Mr. LISTON is "carved out" for dancing, having a light, well-shaped figure, and his terpsechorean efforts are always amazingly relished by his audiences. His great dancing-song is that entitled "The Dancing Swell"; and many a young "swell", during the Christmas festivities, earned great applause by the performance of this unequalled and popular song. After each verse is danced some popular Polka, Redowa, Waltz or Schottische, the whole of the dances being printed in the copy of the song. The melody of the song itself, also, is most captivating, and verily haunts one with its sweetness. It is published with Pianoforte Accompaniment and with Portrait of Mr. LISTON as "The Dancing Swell", at 192, High Holborn, at 3s., and may be had at *half price* of most musicsellers in town and country. Among his other notable Comic Songs may be mentioned "The West End Girls", "The Curly-headed Butcher", "The Pride of Pimlico", "Her Christian Name was Sarah", "The Happy Family" and "Would you if you were me" – all of which have obtained a well-merited popularity.'

Worth quoting as an entertaining sidelight on 19th century publicity jargon! Liston was born in Manchester, started out as a commercial traveller and first appeared on the stage in July 1863 at the Scotia Theatre in Glasgow. His greatest song successes were, in fact, *The convict*, *When Johnny comes marching home* and *Nobody's child*. He was introduced to London by the influential Mr. J. J. Poole, opening at the Metropolitan in 1865, followed by an engagement at the Alhambra. In 1866 he joined Arthur Lloyd's concert party and a year later started a similar group of his own.

HARRY LISTON'S
COMIC SONG BOOK

PRICE SIXPENCE.

MR H. LISTON, FROM A PHOTOGRAPH BY M. ALLEN & CO DUBLIN.

34

"THE FATHER OF THE MUSIC

G. H. McDermott
1845-1933

He was born Gilbert Hastings Farrell and first appeared under that name – so the G. H. is genuine – in spite of which he was generally known as George. After a brief career as a sailor, he took to the fairground booths and the cheaper halls and eventually came into music-hall proper at the Grecian Saloon off the City Road, earlier known as The Eagle (of the famous song). Where the McDermott came from is not quite certain but his success seems to have coincided with the change of name, as so often happens. A talented man who might have become a producer (at which he tried his hand) or a writer. He was responsible for a stage version of Dickens' 'Mystery of Edwin Drood' and wrote a melodrama called 'Racing' which was produced at the Grand Theatre, Islington in 1887. But having a great success in a pantomime at the Grecian, acting, singing and dancing, he was booked for a pantomime 'Bluebeard' at Covent Garden. Caught by the bug and fancying his chances as a dramatic vocalist he acquired the rights to a song called *If ever there was a damned scamp* (which he bought for 10s. 6d.) written by Henry Pettit. The phrase 'damned scamp' caught on and McDermott soon became a popular name in the halls. Another bargain brought him the song *We don't want to fight, but, by Jingo, if we do* (he paid a guinea for that one) and 'Jingoism' became an established word in the English vocabulary while its author, G. W. Hunt, was to be known as 'Jingo' Hunt for the rest of his life. Obviously a potent commentator on current affairs, McDermott also had success with such songs as *Up went the price of meat*, while a nonsense ditty called *I'll strike you with a feather* found much popular favour. Eventually commanding his £100 a week minimum, he became the 'Great' McDermott and lived up to his title with a great show of the grand airs, counterbalanced by a fund of good humour which earned him considerable affection and respect. He made his fortune and topped his career by becoming manager of several theatres, including Forester's off the Mile End Road.

Opposite: Charles Morton by Tom Bourne. The Eagle Tavern.

Arthur Roberts
1852–1933

It would be a somewhat narrow outlook that confined Arthur Roberts (and indeed many who followed in the same mould – Albert Chevalier, Dan Leno, George Robey) to the category of simply 'music-hall artist', for he was a man of wide and varied talents and made a considerable reputation on the stage far beyond the bounds of the 'halls'. He was put on the path of theatrical professionalism by the famous journalist (and erstwhile performer) H. Chance Newton (see his invaluable book 'Idols of the Halls') who knew him first of all as Mr. John Roberts, a young city gent, amateur comic singer with a yen for the theatre. With the name subtly changed to Arthur J. Roberts, Mr. Newton got him his first engagement (fee half-a-guinea) and later wrote him his first successful original song – *If I was only long enough*. After a couple of years or so in this vein, Arthur Roberts took his first steps on the 'legitimate' stage including a period in pantomime during which time he met James Fawn. This led to a double act and Arthur Roberts returned to the music-hall with his new-found partner to sing some ditties which were (in a phrase apparently invented by Mr. Roberts himself) 'very near the knuckle'.

But Arthur Roberts was also one of the first true music-hall comedians, as distinct from the dramatic singers of comic songs that we have looked at so far – a quickfire teller of jokes and droll stories that had the audience rolling about in mirth; he was closely followed by such specialists in this line as R. G. Knowles. It was written in typical Victorian style in 'The Variety Stage' – 'Among eccentric vocalists Mr. Arthur Roberts has so far been unexcelled, but this gentleman has now (1895) seceded from the halls to a more congenial sphere of comic opera and burlesque'. And indeed he had a glittering career in musical comedy and operetta during the 1890s, and in light plays, but he continually returned to his first love and did so until he was very much the 'grand old man' incidentally setting a tradition of longevity that had not been thought of by the earlier stars. As he wrote in the dedication of his rambling and amusing autobiography, 'Fifty Years of Spoof', 'May the last laugh of the oldest clown be the brightest jewel on the youngest crown' – Arthur Roberts provided plenty of jewels.

H. Chance Newton, author of 'Idols of the Halls' (Heath Cranton 1928) photo by Elliott & Fry.

Mr ARTHUR ROBE

ARTHUR ROBERTS

Dedicated to the Tradesmen of England.

CO - OPERATION

(A SONG FOR THE TIMES.)

Co-op, Co-op, Co-op, Co-op, Co-operation Craze,
Go up, go up, go up, go up, the prices still they raise;
They "cop", they "cop", the coppers they "cop" they "cop" in various ways,
They open a shop, and they "cop" "cop" "cop" Co-operation Craze!

WORDS BY
· J. F. McARDLE ·

MUSIC BY
· ALFRED LEE ·

SUNG WITH IMMENSE SUCCESS BY
· ARTHUR ROBERTS ·

Also in the COVENT GARDEN, SURREY,
and all the principal Pantomimes.

PRICE, 3/

ENT. STA. HALL.

LONDON.
· FRANCIS BROS AND DAY (BLENHEIM HOUSE) 351 OXFORD St W ·
PUBLISHERS OF
Smallwood's Pianoforte Tutor, the Easiest to Teach and to Learn from

Jenny Hill and Nelly Power
1850–1896   1853–1887

Nelly Power.   Jenny Hill.

The incursion of the ladies into the music-hall came slowly but surely in the 1860s; that it was a hard and unsuitable life is borne out by the short lives of many of them. Many of the early lady artistes were partners in duos or appeared as 'Serios' but two who began the emancipation toward the times when comic stars like Marie Lloyd were in every way equal to the males were Jenny Hill and Nelly Power who both started as child singers in the 1860s. Jenny Hill was a sharp-witted, bright-eyed girl who quickly gained herself the affectionate title of 'The Vital Spark' She made her debut at a haunt known as the Doctor Johnson Concert Room in Bolt Court off Fleet Street, but she was quickly spotted by an alert agent, Maurice de Frece and booked for the Oxford and the Canterbury. She adopted a line of pathetic humour that touched the heart-strings and tickled the ribs of the patrons at the same time – the hard-done-to wife being a very popular line:

'*He's out on the fuddle with lots of his pals,*
Out on the fuddle, along with other gals;
He's always on the fuddle,
While I'm in such a muddle –
But I mean to have a legal separation.

Jenny Hill as 'The coffee shop gal' photograph by Sarony.

She and Nelly Power shared that classic of the halls *The boy I love is up in the gallery* (a delightfully elegant number). She deserted the halls for a while to appear in Nellie Farren type roles in burlesque at the Gaiety but was glad to get back to the lower humours of the theatrical world that she knew. Later she proved herself an able actress in many roles. A hard life, two or three unsuccessful marriages, eventually extinguished the 'vital spark' and she died only 46 on the 28th June 1896.

The other waver to the boy in the gallery, Nelly Power came in as it were on the back of the success of George Leybourne and the other mashers by being one of the first male impersonators, a forerunner of Vesta Tilley and Ella Shields. It wasn't quite so masculine as later, the dress then was usually tights and spangles, but occasionally she was to be seen in sailor-suit or evening dress taking-off the swells. Her popular songs were *La-di-da* and *Tiddy-fol-fol* and much of her success was due to her sweet and boyish charms in a world of masculinity. She was to die even younger, only 34, after proving herself a 'fascinating and versatile' artiste.

A brief mention here of Bessie Bellwood, another of the tragic beauties, who became famous as one of the first lady singers of Cockney songs, although she began earlier with Irish material. *What cheer 'Ria* of 1887 was one of her great successes. She died of an excess of Bohemian living when only 39 (1857-1896).

James Fawn
1850–1923

CHORUS.
marcato.

If you want to know the time, Ask a P'liceman! The proper Greenwich time, Ask a

Billed as a very minor act on the Middlesex programme in 1880, Fawn was top-of-the-bill in 1883 by virtue of having picked up a good song or two – pre-eminently his long-lasting hit *Ask a policeman* which very quickly caught the public's imagination. In fact, policeman songs seem to have a very special niche in the music-hall repertoire due to the public's obvious pleasure in getting a wisecrack at the 'bobby' in the safety of a gallery seat. Not that there is anything but affectionate humour in the whole of the 'rozzer' literature from about 1840 onwards, though before that they were very unpopular characters. Vance led the way with his *Peter Potts the Peeler* and there was Arthur Lloyd's *Policeman 92X* to mention only two of about 30 policeman songs popular in the 70s and 80s. The policeman literature had two high-class additions to add impetus with the vastly popular *Gendarmes' Duet* in Offenbach's 'Genevieve de Brabant' in 1871 and again in 1880 with 'The Pirates of Penzance'. A delightful and fascinating chapter on the subject is to be found in Christopher Pulling's 'They Were Singing' (Harrap 1952). This diversion is aptly placed under James Fawn's heading because he made a minor speciality of his bobby act and he had several songs in the *Ask a policeman* vein which gave them such good publicity that Fawn was on friendly terms with every policeman in the West End and coughed up many a half-crown tip as he went around with his croney and partner Arthur Roberts. It throws an interesting light on the music-hall's power when it comes to social comment.

Both Arthur Roberts and James Fawn were very funny men indeed, even as solo artists, so they must have been quite a powerful force in partnership. Fawn (née Simmons) started off as a 'nigger' minstrel. Like Roberts he also had a successful career in the other theatre and was very successful in a series of comedies that ran at the Royal Aquarium Theatre in Westminster. We find him described, here and there, as a 'red-nosed comic' (one of the first), 'a bit of a lad' and his principal subject, apart from the policemen, was booze: –

> *'It must have been the lobster, it couldn't have been the wine*
> *For I hardly had enough to drown a fly.'*

he protested without conviction.

G. H. Chirgwin
1854-1922

One of the many music-hall artistes who came from the popular world of nigger-minstrelsy and the seaside concert party was George Chirgwin, who accidentally gained his fame as the 'White-Eyed Kaffir' by rubbing his eye one day just before going on the stage and appearing with a ludicrous white patch in his nigger make-up. This he adapted into a carefully delineated, curious diamond shape which at least made him quite different from all the other 'nigger' impersonators. But he was a remarkable man without this. Excruciatingly thin (he once did a twin act with another thin man Fred Lay in which they sang a song called *We are two skinny wretches*) he was also immensely agile and alight with good humour.

He used the old trick which always seemed to work wonders in the halls of switching from the highly comical to the pathetic and made his biggest hit with a song of true Victorian sentiment called *The blind boy* which inevitably left not a dry eye in the theatre and was as inevitably called for if he ever dared leave it out of the act. Considering that he had a career on the halls lasting for over 40 years it must have been sung quite a few times. Getting thinner and odder as time went on, with his queer make-up and his black tights he must have been a bizarre character. His other great song, featuring his one-string fiddle, was *My fiddle is my sweetheart* which was also heavy with phoney sentiment. At the end of these songs he would break into a strange falsetto voice and then switch, with dramatic suddenness, to a number called *Half a pint of mild and bitter*. Very apt, since when he finally gave up the halls in response to the demands of old age, he took over the Anchor Hotel in Shepperton-on-Thames from 1921, where he was always willing to tell a story or sing a song to help the flow of beer, and happy re-lived his 'Reminiscences'.

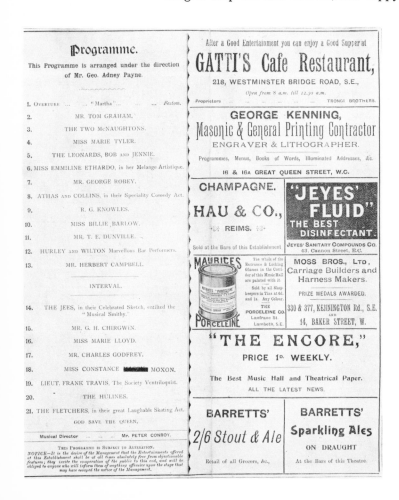

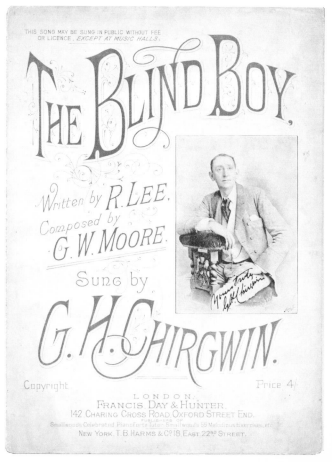

30th Aug. 1881.

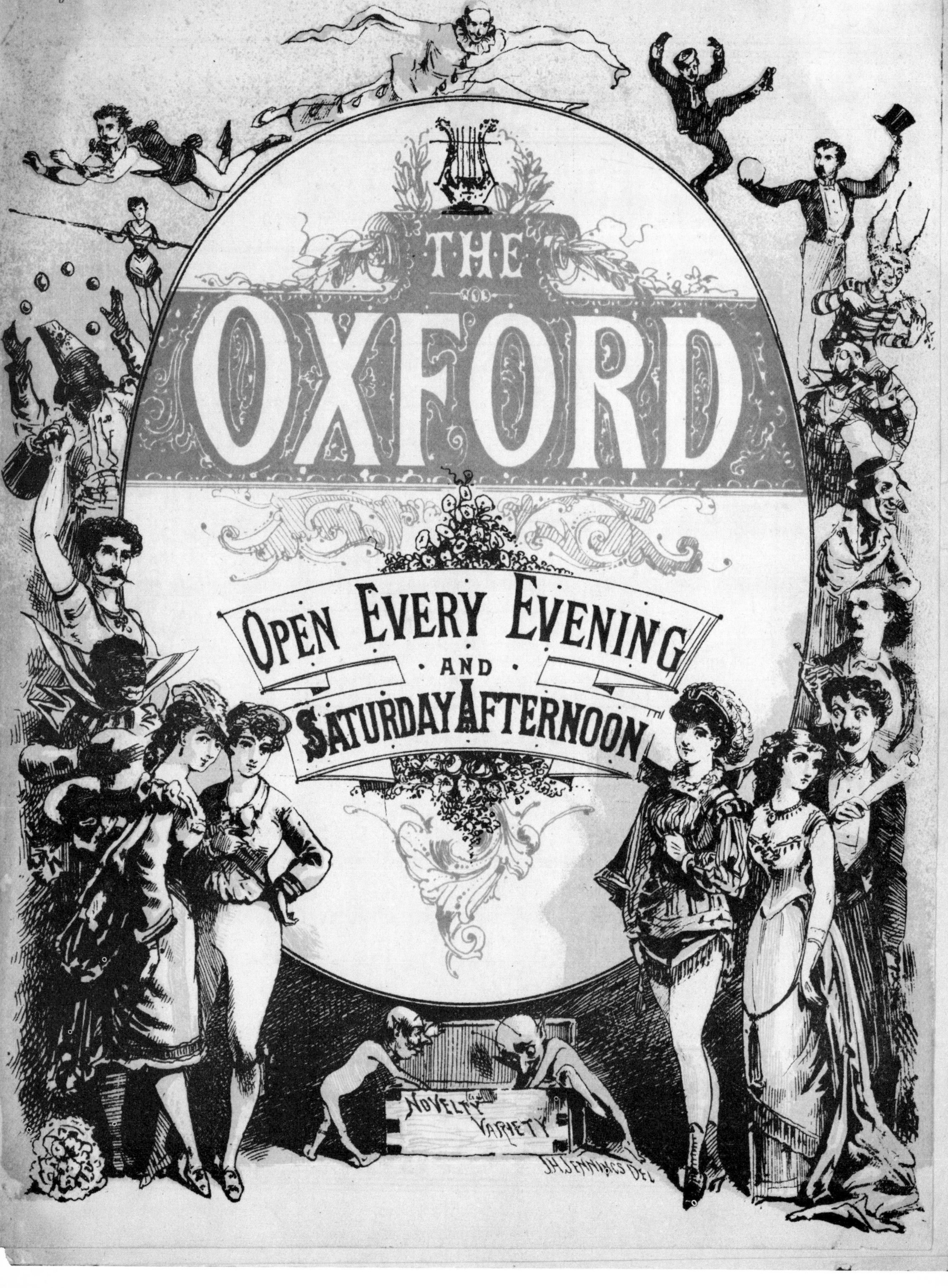

Charles Coborn
1852–1945

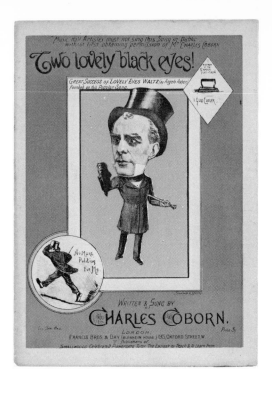

Two lovely black eyes!

GREAT SUCCESS of LOVELY EYES WALTZ (in Angelo Asher)
Founded on this Popular Song

No More Politics For Me

WRITTEN & SUNG BY
CHARLES COBORN.

LONDON.
FRANCIS BROS & DAY (BLENHEIM HOUSE) 195, OXFORD STREET. W

Top left: Charles Coborn as 'The cabby' and 'The Chelsea Pensioner'. *Right:* 'The man who broke the bank', 'Wicked little Mary' and 'Here's another kind of love'.

Two noteworthy attributes, in social terms, that Charles Coborn might possibly be credited with were longevity and respectability – distinctions not often attached to the earlier music-hall performers. It makes his life-story, told in 'The Man Who Broke the Bank' (Hutchinson, n.d.) a fascinating and comprehensive one, ranging from the days of Leybourne and Co. to the 1920s. He was always, as he puts it, 'mixed up in the political side of music-hall business' and had a leading part in forming the Music-hall Artistes Association in 1885 and later helped to make the Music-hall Benevolent Fund a flourishing and useful activity. He was a small but dignified figure, ever ready to back a strike (as happened in 1907) and to criticise those who didn't; much at home in the London Club world, and yet still the trouper with a proper common touch beneath the amusing conceits of his most famous song about the gentleman who did well for himself at Monte Carlo.

The real name was Colin Whitton McCallum, a proud Scottish family, and in his early days he was a clerk. His first earnings as a stage performer was 2/6 for appearing two nights a week at a small music-hall called the Alhambra attached to a public-house in the Isle of Dogs. Already using the name Charles Laurie for amateur dramatics, he finally chose Coborn while discussing the matter with a friend at the corner of Coborn Road in Bow. At the Alhambra he was chairman, manager, vocalist and reciter rolled into one and rose to 2/- a night by moving to the Sugar Loaf Tavern in Whitechapel. After several years of East-ending and touring the provinces the first call to London music-hall proper came in 1879 when he appeared at the Middlesex. Up to now, away from the metropolis, he had sung songs made famous by other stars, but some of his very own became essential and his activities as a composer became of value. Some of the earliest efforts were *Let somebody else have a go, I'm rather too old for it now* and a special line in French songs which he always exploited – one verse of *Monte Carlo* was usually done in the lingo.

Very soon he graduated to top of the bill at the Oxford. The biggest song success so far came with *Two lovely black eyes* in 1886, a parody of an American song called *My Nellie's blue eyes*. This was only ousted in popularity when *The man who broke the bank* was purchased from songwriter Fred Gilbert in 1891. When it was first shown to him he turned it down thinking some of the phraseology a bit hi-falutin' for the halls. During the night he gradually became convinced that he should have bought it and went anxiously to Gilbert's address the next morning fearing he may have lost the opportunity. He first sang it at the end of 1891 and then began to negotiate for publication. Fred Gilbert asked only 10 pounds for his part in it and was paid there and then while Coborn continued to negotiate with Francis, Day & Hunter for the rights. They refused to pay the 30 pounds he demanded but agreed to five pounds down and a royalty. Instead of 30 they eventually paid Coborn some £600.

TWO LOVELY BLACK EYES.

NO MORE POLITICS FOR ME.

Words by CHARLES COBORN.   Arranged by EDMUND FORMAN.

PIANO.

Joseph Tabrar
1857–1931

In amongst our singers of songs we pay tribute to one of the composers of the songs they sang – it was they who provided the means by which the stars rose to fame, and very poorly paid for it most of them were. We choose Joseph Tabrar to represent the forgotten men of music as a typical music hall composer.

Known to the whole music-hall world as 'Joe' he began his own career as a juvenile singer at Evans's Supper Rooms during the reign of the great Paddy Green. While there he often appeared before the Prince of Wales and often received the royal compliments. Thence to the Moore & Burgess Minstrels at St. James's Hall, where he began to write songs and ballads for this celebrated troupe and continued to do so for some 20 years after he had left them. He quickly gained a reputation as a reliable turner of good songs and became a professional song-writer and composer. It seems as if nearly every name in the business called upon his services at some time or another and went away with a good song for a guinea or two. He wrote hundreds of them (his own claim was over 10,000) – songs like *Daddy wouldn't buy me a bow-wow* for Vesta Victoria, *Ting, ting, that's how the bell goes* for George Leybourne, *For months and months and months* for Jack Smiles, *And very nice too* for George Robey, *The ship went down* for Harry Rickards, *Seaweed* for Fred Earle (his son), and so on, and so on – no musical education but a simple facility for the catchy tune

Left. Joseph Tabrar, Fred Earle, Syd Walker.
Right: Joseph Tabrar (in topper) at the trade counter of Francis and Day. c. 1904.

and a knack for low-brow 'poetry':–

'Dearly beloved brethren, is it not a sin
When we peel potatoes to throw away the skin?
For the skin feeds the pigs and the pigs feed you –
Dearly beloved brethren, is it not true?

might be quoted as an example.

But it wasn't only songs – 'Joe' Tabrar would provide anything; jokes, sketches, monologues and he was particularly successful at writing pantomime books. At the height of his career he had a large office and song shop in York Road near Waterloo Bridge, a centre of music-hall trade in those days. His secretary in 1881, so Jimmy Glover recalls in *Hims Ancient and Modern*, was John P. Harrington who later wrote many songs himself and in collaboration with George Le Brunn, including several of Marie Lloyd's songs: Fred Leigh was another of his 'pupils'. 'Joe,' says Glover, 'was a weird sort of chap and was always going to do wonderful things such as knock Sir Arthur Sullivan "into a cocked hat", thoroughly out-do Wagner, and start various heroic adventures which he thought his musical abilities entitled him to do . . . He would write plays or invent patent bottles'. They all knew 'Joe' – so it is rather sad, but true, to read in a learned book on popular song by Sigmund Spaeth which mentions *Daddy wouldn't buy me a bow-wow* that 'the creator of this comic success was a certain Joseph Tabrar, otherwise unsung in Tin Pan Alley!'

In fact it was this brief sentence that set us on the Tabrar trail to discover eventually that his daughter Lily Walker, then in her eighties, was still living in Brixton. She lent us the interesting photographs seen on the opposite page which, in fact, represent a whole 'music-hall' dynasty. Firstly 'Joe' himself, a portrait and seen at the trade counter of Francis, Day & Hunter about 1904; Lily Walker who was on the stage herself; Joe's son Fred Earle (also a composer as well as a singer of ditties); and Lily's husband Syd Walker of 'rags, bottles and bones' immortality.

Harry Randall
1860-1932

'Harry Randall – Old Time Comedian' he called his autobiography and even in 1903 Max Beerbohm was referring to him as an 'anachronism' in the modern halls, which he viewed with displeasure. He started early and first appeared on the stage in 1871 at the Oxford Street Theatre in a drama called 'On the Jury' at 6/– a week. His first professional appearance in a music-hall was at Deacon's Music Hall, which used to be opposite the old Sadler's Wells Theatre in Roseberry Avenue. Almost prostrate with nerves, he nevertheless proved a great success and was called back for two encores and immediately got a contract for a month, the services of an influential agent Hugh J. Didcott and appearances at the Middlesex and Collins. Thereafter Randall was in great demand at the halls, appeared in pantomime (Jenny Hill was one of the stars he worked with and greatly admired). Randall became very much a patter comedian, with the songs used as fillers, and the forerunner of a modern tradition. Most of his musical numbers (which he put over with such great success) have not survived – *It ain't all lavender; Poor Pa paid; I was in it; My wife's a cook; Let 'em all come* and *Oh, what a night it must have been* – all suggestive of a rich material but without the necessary inspired melody to ensure their survival.

An interesting sidelight on names. Harry was accused by an older comedian 'Billy' Randall of pinching the name that he had already made well known. It happened to be Harry's proper name but not Billy's, so there was nothing much he could do about it.

R. G. Knowles
1858-1919

The portrait is familiar; the droll Mr. Knowles in the strange red wig crowned with a seedy old opera hat, long frock coat and baggy white trousers, which he always wore as his visual trademark. All the pictures in books and on song-covers show the lugubrious, Keaton-like face. This was a new kind of comic who told a series of stories at break-neck speed, some of which rather bewildered the audience, pacing restlessly about the stage, speaking in a quick, throaty, somewhat neurotic manner, exhibiting a pained surprise that anyone should actually laugh at him. It was a remarkably effective approach, the stories digging their humour out of the sadder aspects of human existence – of the three marital states, 'love, marriage and divorce', it appeared to be the last which gave him the most pleasure. 'If you want to choose a wife, choose her in the morning early!' was one of his strange bits of advice.

He was decidedly a 'droll' rather than a mere 'comic', Dickensian in appearance, the cheeriness creeping through in the guise of pluckiness rather than outright hilarity, the subjects of his songs being on the lines of *Some things are better left unsaid* and life *On the bench in the park*. It is a line of comedy that has made its mark mostly on the other side of the Atlantic – the Jack Benny artistry is in the same tradition. Knowles was, in fact, a Canadian. He had appeared on stage in America, Chicago 1878, and didn't get to London until 1891 when he appeared at the Trocadero Music Hall.

Herman Darewski in his 'Musical Memories' tells of the interesting personality behind the stage façade; a University lecturer in the States with a vast knowledge of Eastern subjects, cultured, studious, a man with an insatiable curiosity about almost everything. His London flat in Bedford Court Mansions was full of curiosities collected all over the world and he had an intimate knowledge of London life. He was also a keen photographer. He first came to London with his wife who was then appearing on the stage as a banjoist but when she was unsuccessful he again took over the acting chores. Very few people knew of his talents beyond the role of comedian.

Cover of a charity programme at the Pavillion theatre, Glasgow.

Dan Leno
1860–1904

It would be a hard choice to make if one was asked to name a couple of the greatest names in music-hall; but the final choice might well be Dan Leno and Marie Lloyd. Each has come to epitomise a kind of composite music-hall personality; both had talents which impressed themselves unforgettably on all who saw them and have consequently attracted most written attention.

Dan Leno, like so many of the best, did not confine his talents just to the halls. He was certainly one of the most famous pantomime dames of all time; he was a skilled dancer and made his first appearances (as our programme on this page shows) as a champion 'clog-dancer'; he was a fine acrobat, a talented writer of his own material and of a book 'Dan Leno, hys booke' which has something of the literary quality of 'Diary of a Nobody'. His face alone guaranteed his fortune – a comical, tragic, rubbery prop that is almost an archetypal comedians face; full of good humour and yet deeply introspective. His voice, without any imposed exaggerations, was piping and comical and his actions were Chaplinesque in their grace and adroitness. His range of characters were Dickensian in their variety. The titles of some of his songs (although not amongst the top hits)

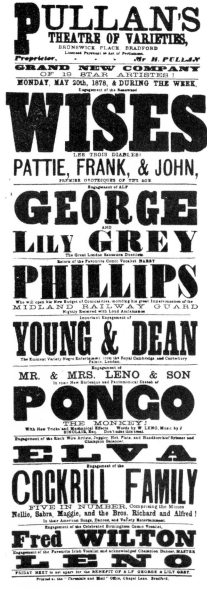

suggest some of his lines – *When Rafferty raffled his watch; The waiter; The good old Tower of London; My wife's mother's gone away; The shop-walker; Our stores;* railway porter, beefeater, every costume photo you see of him impresses itself on the memory, but particularly his female take-offs, nursemaid to lady, and an endless variety of dames, fussy, twittery, sparrow-like ladies of honest vulgarity.

Leno came of theatrical stock. His parents, Mr. and Mrs. Johnny Wilde were a musical turn (their real name was Galvin), but his father died when he was young and his mother married another music-hall performer William Grant who used Leno as his stage name. Dan Leno's first line was acrobat-contortionist with a speciality in Irish songs – his early billing was Dan Patrick Leno; then he appeared as a team with his brother or his uncle Billy Danvers. His first real success was as a dancer, but he soon found his proper metier as a singing comic, starting in the minor London music-halls.

It was a tragically short career. At the end he became mentally disturbed, at times extremely difficult to work with. Harry Randall, who worked with him in the final pantomime, tells of those final days very touchingly in his autobiography.

Tributes abound from the most distinguished of music-hall lovers. Max Beerbohm describes him as 'a sayer of richly grotesque things' with a 'keen insight into human nature' and remembers him particularly in a sketch where he was a shoemaker. All our great comedians have been little, harassed, sad men, immensely lovable and sympathetic, hanging on to laughter as a life-line. 'I defy any one', says Max, 'not to have loved Dan Leno at first sight. The moment he capered on . . . all hearts were his'. He put all rivals in the shade and even the faded photographic portraits show us a character as vivid and likeable as anything in literature or life.

DAN LENO.
JOHNNY DANVERS.   ROTARY PHOTO. CO. LTD
H. CAMPBELL   LONDON E.C.

FORTY THIEVES

I MAY BE CRAZY, BUT I LOVE YOU.

A Mexican Romance,

Written & Composed
by
LESLIE STUART,

Eugene Stratton
1861–1918

Eugene Stratton with Bessie Butt from 'The Music Hall pictorial', *photo:* Denton. Minstrel 'Pony' Moore caricature from 'Entr'acte'.

Well, the 'nigger' minstrel tradition isn't dead yet. In spite of many well-founded protests, our 'black and white minstrels' still draw us to the theatre and glue us to the TV set. So how much more they must have enjoyed the 'darkie' show in the 19th century unhampered by conscience and finer feelings?

Eugene Stratton came to England with the Haverly Minstrels and stayed behind, when they returned, to join the famous Moore and Burgess troupe in their regular stint at the St. James's Hall. He also married the daughter of a great minstrel figure 'Pony' Moore, who founded the company. He soon stood out as a fine singer and dancer and eventually left them to try out his luck on the halls as a solo act with his face its normal white. This didn't produce any results. So he blacked up again and soon had a hit with a song called *The dandy-coloured coon* by George Le Brunn, following this up with *The idler*.

He might have done well with his fascinating soft-shoe-shuffle and this material, but he had better things in store from the moment he met one of England's finest popular song writers, Leslie Stuart. The ex-minstrel and the ex-organist met, became great friends and between them promoted some of the halls' most exquisite songs – well-written, graceful compositions with a long flowing melodic line that never repeats itself: *Little Dolly Daydream; The little octoroon;* and, of course, the finest love song that the stage has known, *The Lily of Laguna.* It is still the song that audiences know and love, and sing best; and its effect is always magical.

As Stratton danced to the oboe strains of the Shepherdess's call, it was, as Macqueen Pope has written, 'not so much dancing as movement expressing the words he had just sung'. It was nothing as brash as tap-dancing, but a completely silent, sinuous movement that had the audience hypnotised. Sometimes he worked in partnership with another fine dancer, Miss Bessie Butt. Well, perhaps this was a sort of sophistication that the early halls never knew, but the sheer artistry overcame those sort of considerations. He was another fine actor, perhaps a better actor than singer, and made a great deal of a tragic song called *I may be crazy, but I love you.*

Sadly, the Stratton-Stuart partnership ended before it needed have done through a trivial quarrel over a horse while they were enjoying their favourite sport of racing. Leslie Stuart went on to his stage successes. He wrote his finest number in 'Florodora' – *Tell me pretty maiden* – and achieved a popular favourite in *The soldiers of the Queen*, written for Victoria's Diamond Jubilee. Stratton repeated the old favourites, at his peak earning some £300 a week; but he died at 57. Stuart frittered his own fortune away and ended a poor man. There is a wonderful record of him playing his own tunes, as he did at the Palladium in 1928; it is to be hoped that someone will revive it on LP before it is too late and all the good copies are lost.

Albert Chevalier
1861–1923

Chevalier's props at 'Queen Hall' *photo:* B. Knight; 'My old Dutch'.

Even Max Beerbohm, 'the incomparable', could be wrong, as people are wrong decade after decade when they allow sentiment and nostalgia to bemuse them into the pitiful cliché 'things aren't what they were' – especially when the inference is that they are not as good as they were. So Max wrote in his famous essay 'The blight on the Music Halls' in *More* (1899): 'the homely humour of James Fawn and Bessie Bellwood was superseded, ere long, by Chevalier, with his new and romantic method; by Gus Elen, with his realistic psychology and his admirably written songs' – entertainments that regrettably taxed his intellect, so he said, rather than entertaining him with the earlier 'fatuous delights'.

This doesn't seem so clear cut to us in 1970: Chevalier and the new method, as compared with Fawn and the old, seem a very fine bit of hair-splitting. Now Chevalier seems and sounds richly in the Cowell and Collins line of dramatics. To hear him singing *My old Dutch* hardly suggests a romantic method as much as a good old bit of Cockney sob stuff. Chevalier had the advantage, or the disadvantage (whichever way you look at it) of 14 years on the legitimate stage with actors like George Alexander before he 'descended' to the halls. He found a vein of gold in a line of coster songs, most of which he wrote himself, but ventured no further with them than to sing them for fellow members at his club. When it was suggested that they would go over well in the music-hall, Chevalier, who liked to think of himself (and by all accounts was) a great dramatic actor, took some persuading. It was mainly the fact that other people started to sing his songs there with great success (*Our 'armonic club* was used by both Charles Coborn and E. J. Lonnen) that persuaded him to invade the Tivoli in 1891. With his 'quaint and semi-pathetic manner' (says H. Chance Newton, who was there) he made a deep impression and had an immediate success. With two songs, wonderfully contrasting and equally memorable, like *Mrs. 'Enry 'Awkins* and *Wot cher!* (or *Knocked 'em in the Old Kent Road*) how could anyone possibly go wrong. With the help of his brother and manager, known on the stage as Charles Ingle, and his pianist Alfred H. West, he produced many more masterpieces: *The little nipper; Our bazaar; The fallen star* and, of course, *My old Dutch*, on which he later based a play and a film which made him a lot of money. Other theatrical ventures were not always so lucrative and he lost a lot of capital in running the Trocadero Music Hall. He still died leaving £7,000 which is great deal more than some of our earlier stars managed.

Perhaps, as he often declared, Chevalier was not, at heart, a music-hall artist but his enormous achievement in this field makes him one of its great personalities. He married Florrie Leybourne, daughter of the 'Great' George. Mr. Beerbohm never quite forgave him for being 'modern' and later wrote (1906) of his 'passion for over-emphasis', of his hammering and 'hamming' points home. Perhaps he was right, but we can hardly dismiss from our annals the man who gave us *Knocked 'em in the Old Kent Road!*

COMRADES.

COMRADES
WALTZ,
BY
GWYLLYM CROWE
MAY
BE HEARD
EVERYWHERE.

Written & Composed
By
FELIX McGLENNON.
Sung with
Immense Success
By
TOM COSTELLO.

Price. 4/.

Tom Costello
1863–1943

'Today, if you look around everywhere, you would not find a man like Tom Costello with songs such as *Comrades* and *At Trinity Church I met my doom*, much less a Marie Lloyd informing you with many a knowing wink that *A little of what you fancy does you good*' – wrote Mr. S. Theodore Felstead in 1944. Quite right, of course, and, had he been writing in 1970, even righter. Those sort of songs may be revived, even copied, but they are not the sentiments or humours that touch the piano-strings of the writers in Tin Pan Alley nowadays. But we wonder why he chose Tom Costello for his pointed remark. Well, partly for the songs which are two imperishable music-hall classics, and partly because Mr. Costello had only just died the previous year, living as many of the stars we mention from now on did, well into an age that could only see them as Victorian relics. The power of that black music, jazz, was too great, too potent for the homely sentiments of Victorian song to survive as a living art.

As Chirgwin was haunted with *Blind boy*, and other stars with their successes, so was Tom Costello with *Comrades*. Whatever else he did or introduced the audience always wanted to hear that song before they were satisfied. His line was mainly the sentimental or patriotic ballad which seemed to fill the coffers all right, but he was capable of full-blooded humour as an occasional flavouring. He had a terrific pull over his audience, moving them to tears with *The ship I love*, then to tears of laughter with *Trinity Church*. He sang them according to the mood of the crowd. He was a real professional, had his great successes as a pantomime dame, and died at the age of 80. But it was always *Comrades*, which sounded a noble song when he sang it, that they wanted in the end.

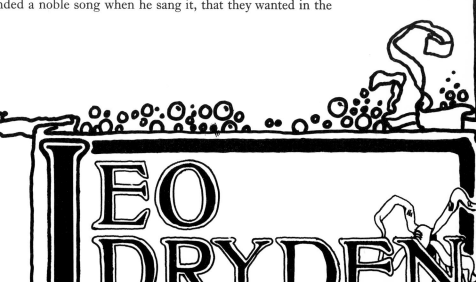

Leo Dryden
1863–1939

Another veteran, born in the same year and living to be 75 was Leo Dryden, born George Dryden Wheeler, a burly individual with a dark moustache, who had a song in similar vein as his piece de resistance – *The miner's dream of home* – 'I saw the old homestead and faces I knew' – as good a pub song as has ever been written. It was nicely burlesqued by Herbert Campbell – 'Pa was boozing nightly and his mother was shifting the gin, while the lodger was taking the old gal out and the old man in', but when Dryden sang it there was hardly a dry eye in the place. He first introduced it at the Oxford Music Hall.

Gus Elen
1863–1940

To call Gus Elen a comic would be stretching the term a little, for all his songs have a touch of sadness about them and a great deal of poetry. His strength was in that he meant every word he uttered: the real tragedy in that most poignant of songs *It's a great big shame*; the unfulfilled ambitions expressed in that beautifully written piece *If it wasn't for the 'ouses in between*; the rather pathetic gaiety of *Down the road*. Gus Elen didn't set out to get laughs, but one laughed with him at the hopeless humour of his situation. Nor was he, in fact, a funny man. He was rather quiet and solemn with none of Dan Leno's sparkling vitality and he didn't come onto the stage grinning or smirking. Occasionally a wide smile would appear when the humour of some situation struck him and then the audience sympathetically smiled with him. The rest of the time one was genuinely moved by this rather sad little Cockney with his rasping little voice that became falsetto with emotion as he sang:

> '*In her hands he's like a little kid –*
> *Oh, I wish that I could get him a divorce.*'

It's a great big shame is one of the great masterpieces of music-hall song, a flawless matching of unforgettable tune and rich and quaint humour. *The 'ouses in between* is perhaps better poetry, but has a few weak points musically. If the authors had originally intended them to be uproariously funny, they eventually got a much better effect when Gus Elen wrung every ounce of pathos from them and sung them with his usual sad, Buster Keaton-like, countenance.

Lesser items in his repertoire included *Seven Dials; Never introduce your donah to a pal; There ain't no getting rid of him at all; The faithless Donah; 'Alf a pint of ale; The golden dustman* – who made a fortune:

> '*Fancy all the dustmen a-shouting in me ear,*
> *Leave us in your will afore you die*'

and all the other songs that made him a great favourite at the Pavilion and other halls.

Perhaps one never knows with a performer of Elen's calibre whether his genius is the result of art or artifice, but certainly in his case one can feel the sincerity coming through even in the recordings that he fortunately left us.

He made a comfortable living out of his art and left £10,000 when he died in 1940. Called back to the stage for a variety performance, one writer recalls the terrific impact he made upon people who scarcely knew of his great days. But the one brief return to glory was enough for him. He happily retired once again to his cottage by the sea to enjoy his hard-earned rest.

IT'S A GREAT BIG SHAME

or

I'M BLOWED IF 'E CAN CALL 'ISSELF 'IS OWN;

Written by
EDGAR BATEMAN.

Composed by
GEO. LE BRUNN.

Vesta Tilley
1864–1952

Vesta Tilley was not the first lady of the halls to make a mark with male impersonations, but she was certainly the greatest. Many who saw her have remarked upon the naturalness with which she did it, wearing the male clothes with such ease and aplomb that she was actually a setter of male fashions in the 1890s. She started the act when she was only four, dressed in male attire and known then as Tilly Ball, daughter of a music-hall chairman in the Midlands. She became variously known as the 'Pocket Sims Reeves' and later the 'Great Little Tilley' before she made her London debut at the Royal Music Hall in Holborn in 1878. From then on she was Vesta Tilley, known as the 'London Idol'. She entranced all who saw her in the music-hall or in pantomime, and had possibly the biggest success in America of any British vaudeville artist who went there.

Wooed by every eligible young man in London, she eventually married a young variety hall manager Walter de Frece, one of a famous theatrical family. He later became Colonel de Frece, M.P., and finally Sir Walter, so that Vesta Tilley ended her distinguished career in a distinguished way as Lady de Frece with a marvellous riverside home in Maidenhead where she wrote her charming memoirs in the 1930s. Her husband also wrote many of her songs.

Apart from her immense vitality and 'boyish' charm, she was particularly perceptive or lucky in finding a number of wonderful songs ideally suited to her special talents. These included *Burlington Bertie* (not to be confused with the gentleman from Bow about whom Ella Shields sung); *Sweetheart May; By the sad sea waves; Following in father's footsteps; Algy, or the Piccadilly Johnny with the little glass eye; Jolly good luck to the girl who loves a sailor;* and her great war-time hit *The Army of today's all right.* In between singing these dashing songs she would show a great dramatic ability with recitations and ballads, one of her 'turns' being an impressive portrayal of the boy poet Thomas Chatterton.

She could be Aladdin and Dick Whittington, she was the perfect 'masher', a tommy, a sailor, an Eastern gentleman, all done with a perfect sense of character, the trim figure beautifully and elaborately attired. After she had visited a provincial town the tailor's shows were assailed for the kind of clothes that Vesta Tilley had worn. In female attire she was just as adorable. Learned critics and penniless young 'clurks' alike fell for her and Mr. Agate noted for us her 'clear enunciation and tiny modicum of a voice'. 'Was there ever such a triumphant storming of an audience', he asks, really misty-eyed.

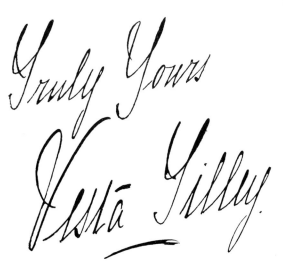

Truly Yours
Vesta Tilley.

Price One Shilling.

FRANCIS & DAYS ALBUM

OF

Vesta Tilley's

POPULAR SONGS.

Together with an Appreciation and
Biographical Sketch by Charles Wilmott.

Contents.

LONDON: FRANCIS, DAY & HUNTER,
142, CHARING CROSS ROAD, W.C.
NEW YORK: T.B. HARMS & FRANCIS, DAY & HUNTER, INC.
1431-3. BROADWAY.

AND OTHER THINGS TOO NUMEROUS TO MENTION,

CHORUS.

My wife's mother is a dear old soul,
    To get rid of her I've tried a new invention,
My motive it is clear, I call her "Mamma dear,"
    And other things too numerous to mention.

CHORUS.

This "Char-mi-ong" young lady was really very nice,
    This "Undressing game" is quite a new invention,
She took off her coat and hat, her shirt and things like that,
    And other things too numerous to mention.

Written, Composed and Sung by

MARK SHERIDAN,

Copyright.

Price 4/-

HOPWOOD & CREW LTD
LATE HOWARD & Cº Music Publishers and Printers, 25 GREAT MARLBOROUGH Sᵗ. LONDON, W.
NEW YORK: W.B. GRAY & Cº 16 WEST 27ᵗʰ STREET.
Copyright MDCCCXCIX in the United States of America, by HOWARD & Cº
H.G.BANKS. Lᵗᴰ.

Mark Sheridan
1867–1918

The trend toward looking as well as being funny came in with our next three artistes, Mark Sheridan, Little Tich and George Robey, each of whom added an unforgettable trademark in eccentric attire. With Mark Sheridan it was those ridiculous bell-bottom trousers which would perhaps be regarded as a mark of fashion nowadays, though his were slightly "beller"-bottomed, as one can see from the song-sheets. He had a line in coy humour, some excellent songs like *Who were you with last night* and *I do like to be beside the seaside*, and a good, resounding voice to sing them with.

He was a great one for having a go at the audience, getting them to insult him and then giving them twice as good as he got. Perhaps the ridiculous garb – black frock coat, topper, curious workman's trousers, tight round the knees and flaring out at the bottom like inverted flower-pots, and usually an umbrella or a stick in his hand – was subconsciously intended to invite comment. It did the trick.

During the First World War, Mark Sheridan was particularly successful in finding a number of songs which hit the comic-patriotic vein that has made the 'poetry' of that miserable conflict endure. *Here we are, here we are, here we are again* proved to be a marching song second only to *Tipperary* and *Pack up your troubles*. *Belgium put the kybosh on the Kaiser* may have been prematurely optimistic, but it went down well at the time. He had a good line in dramatic songs like *The villain still pursued her* and did everything with tremendous power and pace, including an act that foreshadowed the very successful act of our beloved Richard Hearne, in which he danced a quadrille by himself.

The end was tragic. Suffering a nervous breakdown he began to feel that he was losing his touch and shot himself in a Glasgow park.

Little Tich
1868–1928

The real name was Harry Relph and as such he first appeared at the Rosherville Gardens near Gravesend in 1880. His first appearances in the London music-halls were as a black-faced comedian and he began to call himself 'Little Tichbourne' after a certain famous figure of the time. The eccentricity that made his name was an incredible dance performed in enormous boots on which he raised himself up to more or less normal height by standing on the tips. A gnomish little fellow with a persistent grin, he really was very small and after he had become 'Little Tich' the word 'tich' slipped into the English language.

He really doesn't slip into our annals as a singer, for songs were only an incidental part of his act, his best perhaps being *All over the shop*. But one couldn't leave out such a famous figure. His portrayals of odd characters – a miniature Sergeant-Major; a Spanish dancer (female); a jockey (a natural) – and his amazing acrobatic violence – always taking impossible falls, whacking himself with a stick – made his whirlwind act unforgettable. He was an accomplished linguist and a marvellous impersonator, but it is visually that we shall really remember him in those big flapping boots that were nearly as long as he was tall.

Harry Champion
1866–1942

'*Any old iron, any old iron, any-any-any old iron;*
You look sweet, you do look a treat,
You look dapper from your napper to your feet . . .'

When Rudyard Kipling wrote 'The music-hall song is a necessary part of our civilisation . . . and may even come back again' he might well have had the art of Harry Champion in mind. They certainly had much in common. Harry Champion added his fair quota to the quotable and quoted phrases that music-hall has given to the English language . . . 'any old iron', 'boiled beef and carrots' and his 'wot'cher'. He probably did more for the reputation of 'Henery the Eighth' than the authors of any history book. Harry as you can see from the photograph taken when he was actually recording *Henery the Eighth*, was the archetypal man in the pub – a paunchy, horse-faced, red-nosed, loud but likeable fellow, fill of good tips, bad beer and his 'weskit' stained with cheap good living.

Rather surprisingly Harry Champion set out on his stage career as a black-faced comedian, then known as Will Conway. He first appeared in a London music-hall in 1888 at the Queen's Poplar, a long-flourishing establishment originally known as the Apollo Music Hall. He soon won the affections of his audience by conjuring up for them various imaginary meals, for he was one of the most culinary comedians we have had, offering, in addition to *Boiled beef and carrots*, songs about *Hot tripe and onions, Hot meat pies, savaloys and trotters* and other homely dishes – all washed down with a pint at *The old Red Lion* and rounded off with a fat cigar. A Falstaffian figure preoccupied with good but bargain-priced living.

His songs were hardly subtle. Mostly written by the same team of song writers, they sound remarkably alike not only in sentiment but in melody. But that was part of the essential, immediately recognizable style. His voice was not a particularly musical one, but his diction was amazing. He could pack in more words a minute and more songs per turn than anyone else on the stage.

He became very popular at the Old Middlesex Hall (known as the Old Mo), the last of the great 'red-nosed' comics. Picture his whirlwind act as he dashed on the stage, shouted out his songs in that wheezy old voice, one after the other, all accompanied by hectic gesticulations – a stock-type that many have since tried to copy. 'It was quite fascinating', writes Mr. Felstead, 'to watch and hear him rattling off those idiotic songs at express speed; you kept wondering when he would ever get a word wrong'. He seldom did.

Left: Harry Champion recording 'Henery the Eighth'.

George Robey
1869–1954

The music-hall figure that 1969 chose to centenarise most wholeheartedly was George Robey – hardly surprising for someone who attained the title of 'Prime Minister of Mirth'. Robey's songs were in a very personal comic vein, slightly arch, full of social comment, naughty but precise, and had long, Victorian titles which were their oft-repeated punch lines, like *I stopped, I looked, I listened* and *Bang went the chance of a lifetime.* Some of the remarks made in them would be equally applicable today, as in *It wouldn't surprise me a bit* when he came round to the observation that if all the railway fares went up once again – well, it wouldn't surprise anyone a bit.

The George Robey that remains in the mind's eye is the bishop-like figure with the flattish pork-pie hat, the collarless coat, all soberly black, with the Chaplinesque stick and the enormous eyebrows which were nearly all as nature supplied them. The cherubic-cum-priestly appearance and the cultured voice (which belonged to a man of considerable learning and taste) were a perfect foil to the very near-the-knuckle humour. But it was the audience who got the blame as George raised the big eyebrows in surprise at their taking the wrong meaning from his careful double-entendres. On stage he was very calm and had no need to be wildly active. He would just stand there and talk and ad lib.

The 'prime-ministerial' act was very far from being his only one, however. He was a great character actor and we are familiar with pictures of him in all manner of strange guises. Nor was his ability confined to the music-hall. As the star of a number of highly successful musical comedies and revues, he will always be connected with a very great song *If you were the only girl in the world* by Nat D. Ayer which he sang with Violet Loraine in 'The Bing Boys are Here' in 1916. It slipped into the act later, but was not primarily a music-hall song. His acting took him into straight plays and he made a memorable Falstaff on stage and screen. One of his last film parts was as Sancho Panza to Fedor Chaliapin's Don Quixote. As a prehistoric man, a mayor, as Oliver Cromwell or Sir Walter Raleigh, Robey was very capable of slipping into a convincing part – and, of course, he made a wonderful pantomime dame.

But still we shall always see him as almost the archetypal music-hall artiste, the prim penguin-like figure set in the framework of the footlights and the proscenium; modesty outraged as he tried to quieten the outrageous laughter with a pained 'Desist'; or, at some particularly hysterical moment – 'I'm surprised at you!'. This only made matters worse as he admonished them with genuine pained surprise in the final reproach 'I haven't come here to be laughed at' and ultimately appealed to the management. All was done with masterly economy of movement and a twist of those ridiculous eyebrows which alone were sufficient to identify him on a poster.

Archibald, certainly not, may not be a great song but it is a very personal one. Actor, writer, artist (he would always sign an autograph book with a little drawing of himself), a scholar, a good athlete, a maker of violins and a musician – but above all the 'Prime Minister of Mirth'.

Bransby Williams
1870–1961

'IS PIPE.

WRITTEN BY
CHAS H. TAYLOR.

COMPOSED BY
CUTHBERT CLARKE.

Amongst the singers of songs, the funny gentlemen and ladies, let us slip in someone who represents the ever-widening scope of the halls. From earliest times, character acting had been a major part of music-hall entertainment from Sam Collins, via Chevalier and Leno, to Robey and Lauder. When Mr. Barnes, manager of the Shoreditch Theatre, slipped in, as an extra turn, a young man who simply did a dramatic monologue and was a sensational success, he helped lead the steps of Bransby Williams toward being a figure of the halls rather than another Henry Irving of the legitimate stage. If he was only a great 'ham' actor in the end, he struck a vein of powerful exaggeration that really had the audience gripped with its magic even though they knew that they were being had. Even today a piece like *The green eye of the little yellow god* has very much more cynical audiences half held with its tragedy and only half daring to laugh.

His special line, which has been exploited many times since by great actors like Emlyn Williams, was the impersonation of Dickens characters, larger-than-life affairs, but with just the right mixture of pathos and humour to appeal to a music-hall audience. A big, impressive man, whose first intentions were to become a missionary, he started out in repertory but soon claimed his unique place as the actor of the halls. From his first Shoreditch appearance in 1896 he caught the public's fancy with his impersonations of Henry Irving, Beerbohm Tree, Charles Wyndham and other great actors of the day. He was soon fully engaged at all the major halls including the Tivoli, where he was a special favourite. His Dickens roles, starting in 1897, included Micawber, Heep, Sykes, Fagin, Pecksniff, Carton, Jingle and Mrs. Gamp and Buzfuz. Next he introduced his dramatic monologues which, in addition to the famous *Green eye*, included such tear-jerkers as *How we saved the barge; For a woman's sake* and *The Yogi's curse*.

Later, notably in the 1920s, he toured with his own company in dramatisations of Dickens, in Shakespeare and in other plays, here and abroad, returning to the variety stage again in 1929. He lived and worked to a grand old age, rounding off his career with several films.

Nellie Wallace
1870–1948

Ada Reeve tells in her book of memories 'Take It For a Fact' of her appearance in 1894 in the pantomime *Jack and Jill* at the Comedy Theatre in Manchester. Her understudy and Second Girl was Nellie Wallace, who finally took over when Ada had to depart for family reasons. 'She had not', says the authoress, 'developed her own distinctive style at that time, but was still trying to compete with prettier girls in ordinary show business'. Certainly nobody would describe Nelly as a beauty. She had the appearance of a troubled hen, but it was her skinny vivacity and outraged looks that led her into the ways of music-hall humour.

She had made her first appearance on the music-hall stage, in fact, in 1888 in Birmingham as a clog-dancer, in which role she was known as 'La Petite Nellie'. Then she joined in a family affair as one of the Three Sisters Wallace touring halls all over the country. Not finding any particular success, she turned to drama, comedies and pantomime, where Ada Reeve discovered her. Finally she found her metier as a solo turn and became a star of the halls with songs such as *I was born on a Friday* and *I lost Georgie in Trafalgar Square*.

How much of our British humour depends on the strained mirth of the down-trodden! Nellie Wallace, a droll little spark of a woman, a sort of female Dan Leno, gave into the fact that her curious features were not packed with allure. In her equally strange, rapid voice she told of many romances that went wrong or hardly got started at all. Her attempts to be posh amounted to her little bit of ragged fur – 'me bit of vermin' – and a flowery hat, and an unflagging outraged dignity. She had a great gift for characterisation, a broadly vulgar sense of humour (one of her funniest acts was as a washerwoman ironing a pile of the type of garments that should not be seen or mentioned in public) and an endless flow of patter. Later she became the best of the female pantomime dames – a fine Widow Twankey, and fine comedy actress of great ability. But she was mainly Nellie Wallace.

Kate Carney
1870–1950

Kate Carney was described by James Agate, who saw her at the Alhambra in the 1920s as 'the last of the great *lionnes comiques*' – a surviving purveyor of the grand manner. A female Robey who held the stage with the merest flick of the hand, a trivial gesture, she could convince you with the simplest of props that she was an orphaned child or a forsaken lover, and jerk the tears accordingly. *Are we to part like this, Bill* was her great number which never failed to move, though on paper it hardly moves into the realms of great literature.

She was a buxom lass, a true Cockney Queen, a flower-seller type who addressed everyone as 'duck' or 'love'. Her other songs were mainly in praise of low-class London life, and she sang them with great simplicity and feeling. Her *Liza Johnson* was a faithful girl with an inarticulate but jealous lover; her chief delight two-pennorth of fish and chips on a Saturday night and a nice new hat to wear.

ARE WE TO PART LIKE THIS ?

Written & Composed by
HARRY CASTLING
and
CHARLES COLLINS

Immortalised by
KATE CARNEY

LONDON · ENGLAND:
B. FELDMAN & CO. LTD
125, 127, 129, SHAFTESBURY AVENUE W.C.2

COPYRIGHT

ROLAND'S PIANOFORTE TUTOR THE BEST IN THE WORLD
ENGLISH FINGERING   CONTINENTAL FINGERING

2/-

It's a Bit of a Ruin that Cromwell Knocked About a Bit.

Words by
Harry Bedford
and Terry Sullivan.

Music by
HARRY BEDFORD.

Sung by
MISS MARIE LLOYD.

Copyright. LONDON, ENGLAND. Price 2/- net

B. FELDMAN & Cº., Lᵀᴰ 125, 127, 129, Shaftesbury Avenue, W C.2.

Marie Lloyd
1870–1922

The Queen of the Halls was, of course, Marie Lloyd. Her centenary in 1970 was rightly marked with eulogies in all the highbrow papers, programmes on television and wireless, and even a musical which perhaps rightly but nonetheless disappointingly made little use of her songs. She was born appropriately in Peerless Street, Hoxton and her real name was Matilda Alice Victoria Wood. Nicknamed Tilly, she was called Marie by her own choice. She was one of a talented family of girls, all of whom had considerable success on the stage but were outshone, unfortunately for them, by the inimitable Marie. Her first appearance was aptly at the famous Eagle in the City Road in 1885, where she was billed as Belle Delamere; but on her second appearance there it was as Marie Lloyd, the surname being borrowed from 'Lloyd's Weekly News' and the result a name that everyone could and did remember.

MARIE LLOYD.

PRINCIPAL GIRL, RED RIDING HOOD.
SOLE AGENT, THE OLD RELIABLE, GEO. WARE.
FROM THE ENTR'ACTE ANNUAL OF 1892

Her first song was borrowed from earlier music-hall days (Nellie Power was one of its singers) – *The boy I love sits up in the gallery;* this she sang with great simplicity and tenderness. But like all the great stars she could move with incredible ease from being a shy girl to a grand lady of considerable dignity or a disreputable old ruin, one of the ones that Cromwell knocked abart a bit. But it was the rather naughty, toothy, slyly winking Marie that used to get them most of all with songs like *Then you wink the other eye; Twiggy-voo; A little of what you fancy does you good* and her greatest hit *Oh, Mr. Porter*, with its candid and inviting confession of 'what a silly girl I am'.

Not unnaturally Marie Lloyd has drawn tribute from distinguished pens. Mr. James Agate described her 'expressive dial' in terms too deep for the ordinary music-hall patron when he tells us that she had 'the *petite frimousse évéille*, the wideawake little "mug" which Sarcey noted in Réjanee' – but we get a hint of what he meant. She depicted the low life, the humble, the vulgar, with technical perfection. Using her exquisite hands and feet, she 'expounded those things which she knew to be dear to the common heart'. Even so austere a writer as T. S. Eliot devoted an essay to her. He summed her up as 'the most perfect, in her own style, of British actresses', not a 'grotesque' (among whom he regarded Little Tich and Nellie Wallace), but all real person, never in defiance of an audience, but always sure of having them on her side, knowing, because her sympathy was full and discerning, just how every type of woman she portrayed would act in the circumstances. Max Beerbohm and many others have wondered at her artless art.

Well, that was the stage. Her own life was not entirely happy. She had three husbands. The second, Alex Hurley, was a well-known figure of the music-halls himself; the last, a jockey, helped her to spend the money which she had not already given away with typical generosity. Her last appearance, now desperately ill, was at Edmonton and the last song she sang was *One of the ruins that Cromwell knocked about a bit.* Two nights later she died and after the funeral more than 100,000 people filed past her grave and felt that a universal light had gone out. She was always 'Our Marie' to highbrow and lowbrow alike.

Harry Lauder
1870–1950

Harry Lauder was the eldest of seven children. The family was poor and when his father died while Harry was only 11 he was forced to take part-time employment in a coal-mine, earning 10s. a week. To supplement this, he tried his hand at entertaining, singing at the local harmonic society gatherings and sometimes earning £1 a night for his already outstanding talents. Some of the songs he sang were folksongs, some he wrote himself.

He was soon engaged for a few weeks tour of music-halls in the North of England and, bang full of self-confidence right from the start, he gave up the mines and headed for London. His first appearance was at Gatti's in Westminster Bridge Road, where he sang *Tobermory* and *Killicrankie* with immediate success. The engagement, at £7 a week, was won by luck and self-assurance, but immediately all the music-hall managers were after him and he had contracts for 300 weeks work at £10 a week. Not many of those contracts lasted out a year as Lauder became one of the most sought after of all music-hall stars, eventually earning £1000 a week at the Pavilion Theatre in Glasgow.

His first great song was *I love a lassie*. This he sang in one of his infrequent appearances in pantomime, 'Aladdin' at the Theatre Royal, Glasgow in 1905, and demand for it never ceased from thereon. Five years later he wrote *Roamin' in the gloamin'* for another pantomime and this was just as popular. He was to write hundreds of songs eventually, but none to equal these two.

Harry Lauder, knighted in 1919 for his ceaseless work for the troops and raising money for charity during the First World War (he wrote a book called 'Minstrel in France') was a complete master of stage craft. His songs and his characterisations were rehearsed to perfection before being allowed on the stage; through calculated effect he achieved a confident naturalness. He had, said James Agate, 'the great artist's overweening conceit of himself;' he emerged 'from the wings like the sun from base clouds'. Positively enraptured by Lauder, Agate compared him extravagantly with Munden, Wordsworth and Irving; slight and mundane as most of Lauder's songs were, seen in cold print, they were given 'spontaneous and magical effect' when he sang them.

He was a short, not particularly handsome man, with rough hair, bowed legs which the inevitable kilt emphasised, and he revelled in his physical shortcomings. He was full of humanity and enjoyed, as he said himself, 'playing on the heartstrings of men and women'. His sketches were full of detailed observation of character, his timing was perfect, his variety endless. He had a splendid baritone voice and, in the tradition of George Leybourne, would surprise his audience with a ballad like *Rocked in the cradle of the deep*. He lost his son during the War, but all that he saw at the front made him determined not to 'give way to grief'. He was a great star until the end and became a very rich man, cultivating the legend of Scottish 'thriftiness' but giving generously. The very titles of his songs – beside the two great ones mentioned – recall the voice which was fortunately amply recorded: *She is ma daisy; Stop yer ticklin' Jock; Just a wee deoch-an-doris; It's nice to get up in the morning;* and that great emotion ringer which typified his own philosophy of life – *Keep right on to the end of the road.*

stop yer tic-kle-ing— tic-kle-ic-kle-ic-kle-ing— stop yer tick-ling, Jock!" "Will you Jock!"

Fine.

D.C.

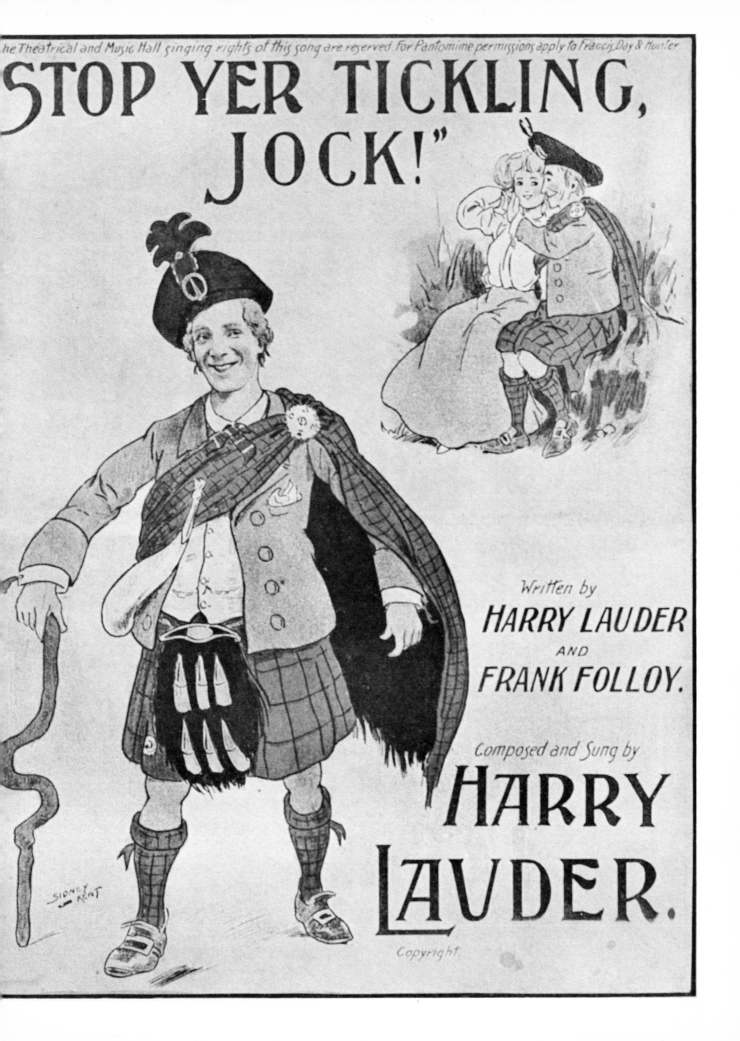

Marie Kendall
1873–1964

Marie Kendall was five when she made her first stage appearance at the Pavilion in the Mile End Road. By the 1890s she was top of the bill at the Alhambra and earning the princely sum of £20 a week. Macqueen-Pope described her as 'tall, handsome and distinguished', and so she remained. She was in the first Royal Variety Show in 1912 and appeared again, already nearing sixty in 1932. By then she had found her great song, *Just like the ivy*, which she reckoned to have sung some 5,000 times since the first time she pleased a music-hall audience with it in 1902. Her comedy was as graceful as her presence, her songs were sweetly sentimental.

Kendall remained a name to be reckoned with in show business for many years. Her son Terry and daughter Pat followed her into the halls with a dancing act; and her beautiful grand-daughter Kay Kendall became a famous actress and film-star. When Marie died at her home in Clapham she had just turned 90.

Ada Reeve
1874–1966

Right: Auditorium of the Alhambra, demolished in 1936.

Ada Reeve was a woman of many parts and became known to us as a talented film actress as well as a great stage comedy actress. Most of her career belonged to the musical comedy theatre in such shows as 'The Gay Parisienne', 'Milord Sir Smith', 'The Shop Girl', 'Florodora', 'San Toy', 'The Medal and the Maid' and 'The Dubarry', to mention a mere handful, and she was a regular star of pantomime. Marie Kendall was her 'attendant sprite' when she played Fairy Kindness at the Whitechapel Pavilion way back in 1884. And yet her comparatively brief appearances on the real music-hall stage, particularly at the earlier stages of her career, marked her as a great music-hall artiste.

Her first engagement was at The Middlesex, billed as 'The Juvenile Wonder' and thereafter, a veteran of 14 and 15, she appeared in several East End Halls, finally coming back to the West End as a star attraction with a perky line in feminine songs such as *I'm a little too young to know*. The Tivoli, the Metropolitan, where she first sang *What do I care*, the Canterbury – all enjoyed her talents, and in 1893 she had a successful tour of America. Thereafter the musical stage took her time mainly, but she was frequently back in the music-halls. George Gamble in 'The Halls' describes her: 'clever almost beyond compare; she is fragile and dainty; she is fine and delicate. Her singing is pleasant: it is so distinct and well-managed. Her dancing is delightful: it is so unforced and floating . . . there is no woman on the music-hall stage who possesses a greater range from grave to gay . . . she can be suggestive without being offensive, pathetic without being funny, funny without being pathetic'. No wonder she went on to 'higher' things.

Harry Tate
1873–1940

A music-hall trademark that became as famous as Robey's eyebrows, was Harry Tate's precarious moustache. Outrageously false and mobile, it was almost convincingly a part of him, so much did it give to the partnership. Off stage Harry Tate was a kindly, lovable man and the little troupe of actors who helped him in the famous sketches stayed with him for most of his career. He was never, on the stage or off, suggestive or vulgar – just genuinely, uproariously funny, the very spirit of burlesque. He was the forerunner of a line of comedians who are always in trouble, optimistic to extremes, full of bright schemes that ever go astray, a silent-screen type brought to life on the music-hall stage.

It was the sketches, carefully contrived, unpredictably disastrous, that made Tate a new kind of star. The most famous was *Motoring*, a classic of accumulative chaos. The number of things that happened to him in such a short space of time was amazing. The people around, including a rather nasty little son who received most of the parental wrath, a policeman and several unhelpful bystanders, worked him up into mountains of exasperation. At last he was in the car, put it into gear and waved goodbye – but nothing happened.

Just to describe the sketches is hardly likely to reproduce the glorious atmosphere of helpless laughter which they engendered. There was *Fishing*, in which other anglers were the target of his fury; the *Office* sketch with a particularly nasty office boy; *Billiards*, an epic of frustration; *Golfing*, which inspired many copies; *Peacehaven*, in which Tate tried hard to be the retired country gentleman; and hilarious epics which incorporated the grim warfare of man with wireless, telephone, aeroplane, motor-bike. His invention was endless and hilarity was guaranteed.

It was a very English type that he created – the earnestly dedicated, snobbish Englishman who always had to dress right (usually *over*dress right) and have everything and everybody organised. All who thwarted him or pricked his dignity were described as 'common'; what he thought of all the disasters, only he and the moustache knew. His self-control was terrific until he lost it, then exasperation reigned supreme. He was probably the most outrageous funny man that music-hall has known. It was enough to make a Queen laugh – and it did. Music was not much a part of Harry Tate's act but he had one or two good songs which have been remembered – *Good-byee*; and, quite a catchphrase in its time, *How's your Father*? He was killed during an air-raid in 1940 and the world has never been quite such a funny place since.

Vesta Victoria
1874-1951

The two ladies on this page were two of music-hall's most successful representatives of the 'weaker' sex, earning fantastic salaries in their prime and between them – perhaps the great secret of their success – owning more memorable songs than any other dozen you care to mention. Vesta Victoria, daughter of Joe Lawrence who used to manage the Empire at Cardiff, was very much in the tradition – vivacious, naughty, with a voice of plummy dignity that made a very great deal of slight material. She was small and lively and, like the very best stars, knew how to bend an audience to her will. It was that silliest of songs, *Daddy wouldn't buy me a bow-wow* (written by Joseph Tabrar) which she invested with coy assurance, that became her biggest hit. Her songs were always full of character and include some of the best-turned numbers we have had – or was it Vesta who made them so when she 'struck a light', as one publicity punster put it? There are sterling qualities in her renderings of *Waiting at the Church; He calls me his own Grace Darling; It's all right in the summer time; Now I have to call him Father* and the classic *Poor John.*

It was said of her: 'She is vivacity itelf. Her power of enlivening is great. She is provocative, but amusing. Although she may not always please, she will rarely offend. She may sometimes disturb; but she will never bore.' Her favourite remark, records Georgie Wood, was: 'Now isn't that a coincidence'. As she said to Blyth Pratt, manager at the Oxford: 'So you haven't changed your funny name and I haven't changed mine – isn't that a coincidence'. A delightful comedienne, indeed, who could make the most of promisingly naughty material (dressed in prim white frock and black stockings and shoes) such as *Our lodger's such a nice young man!*

Florrie Ford
1874-1941

The second of our record-holding hit singers came from Melbourne – née Flanagan, oddly enough, in view of one of her hit songs. She ran away from home for the lure of the theatre when she was 14. On her first appearance in Sydney she shocked a prudish manager by singing: 'He kissed me when he left me, and told me to be brave'; he demanded something less suggestive for the following night. In 1897 she was heard in Australia by G. H. Chirgwin who advised her to come to England, which she did, making the Derby Castle at Douglas in the Isle of Man one of her favourite venues.

Her choice of songs was inspired. She refused to pay more than £25 for the rights to any of them and if the audience didn't pick up the chorus on the first hearing, they were discarded. And what a choice she made! One of the first to sing *It's a long way to Tipperary*, her list is full of evocative memories. *Down at the old Bull and Bush; She's a lassie from Lancashire; Oh, oh, Antonio; Hello, hello, who's your lady friend; Has anybody here seen Kelly; Hold your hand out, naughty boy; Flanagan* (take me to the Isle of Man again); *Pack up your troubles in your old kit bag* – she seems to have provided half the munitions to win the First World War. By a quirk of fate, she died one evening during the Second World War, having spent the afternoon singing for the troops in a naval hospital. There have been few artistes of comparable verve and impact. A fellow Australian, Dame Nellie Melba, always maintained that Florrie Forde had the voice and ability to become a great opera singer – but happily she did no such thing.

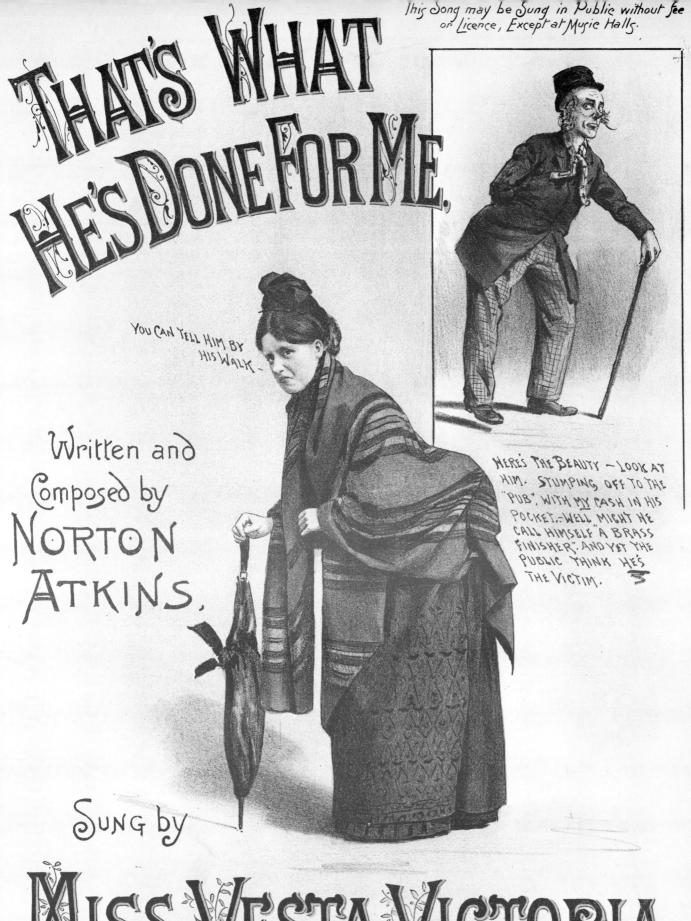

THE PAVILION

RENFIELD ST
SAUCHIEHALL ST

GLASGOW

Sole Proprietors, THE GLASGOW PAVILION LIMITED

Manager - - - - Mr. EVAN GOOD.

6-50—TWO PERFORMANCES NIGHTLY—9

MONDAY, 29th SEPTEMBER, 1913, and during the Week.

☞ FREE LIST ENTIRELY SUSPENDED. ☜

EXCLUSIVE ENGAGEMENT OF THE POPULAR COMEDIAN—MR.

WILKIE BARD

In his Latest London Successes including "CHRYSANTHEMUMS," or A Lesson to Husbands at 4 a.m.
This is Mr. BARD'S absolute Last Appearance in this Country, prior to his departure for America.

LUCY LYND, Lancashire Comedienne

HELENE & EMILON

In their Great Original Novelty Gymnastic Act.

SPECIAL NOTICE.

There will be a GRAND SPECIAL MATINEE, MONDAY, 29th SEPT., 1913 (Autumn Holiday)
SAME PROGRAMME AS EVENING.
Doors open at 2. Commence at 2-30.

Miss MAY LILIAN LEVEY

The Popular Pantomime "BOY," in Comedy Chorus Songs.

MARGIT & LENER

The Clever Eccentric Pair. Comedy Acrobats. In a Refined Eccentric Act, "WET PAINT."

ALF BROOKES, Character Patter Comedian

Introducing his Novelty Football Song and Latest Chorus Hits.

JESSIE

BROUGHTON

Principal Contralto (from the Apollo, Daly's and Gaiety
Theatres, London, etc., etc.)
and DENNIS

Welcome Return of

MDLLE.

MARGO

Wilkie Bard
1874–1944

Born William Augustus Smith, which would not have done at all, and starting out in life as a clerk in a textile firm in Manchester, Wilkie Bard started entering amateur talent contests, where his distinctive voice added such sparkle to the songs he sang that he inevitably won. The promoters of these competitions got a little tired of his perpetual success and said that he 'ought to be barred'. He took the hint and a name appropriately odd enough for his own odd character. As a professional he did the rounds of the North and West country halls before coming to London and making his first appearance at Collins'.

In spite of his origins it was as a Coster comedian that he first made his name, an indication of his skill at portraying every kind of character. He was particularly good at female impressions, a charlady or a landlady; but he also had a good line in policemen, watchmen and other homely types. Most of his songs were based on character studies: the long-haired, contemplative gentleman who told them *I want to sing in opera*, or the constable – *I'm here if you want me*. He had two great successes with the tongue-twisting *She sells seashells* and with the timely song on the subject of suffragettes – *Put me on an island where the girls are few*. He was a great stylist, a fine professional and, at his peak, was earning £650 per week in America and rarely less than £250 in England, all with good clean comedy and an eye for the human details that mould character. He worked till the end and died happily in his sleep.

"PUT ME UPON AN ISLAND."

(WHERE THE GIRLS ARE FEW.)

Written & Composed by
WILL LETTERS

Arranged by
J. CHAS. MOORE.

Billy Merson
1881–1947

Real name William Henry Thompson, he was born in Nottingham and, schooldays over, was put to work in the telephone service. Being a natural acrobat, he did the traditional thing by running away from home to join a circus and became an excellent clown called Ping Pong. Next as a partner in an act called Keith and Merson he tried the halls, first appearing in variety in Birmingham in 1900. When jobs were hard to get the pair took to piano-tuning, about which they knew nothing at all.

Eventually W. H. T. decided to become a solo turn, having a yearning to appear in gentlemanly guise in top hat and tails after years of red-nosed clowning, so he and his partner tossed for names and Billy got the Merson half. Now as Billy Merson he came to London and made his first appearance there at the Middlesex in 1905. Having an excellent voice and considerable acting as well as athletic ability and a great sense of humour he soon became well known for his character songs, early ones being *Setting the village on fire*, *A prairie life for me* (where he milked the cows for the Maypole dairy) and *The photo of the girl I left behind me*, all modest successes. His big hit came with a song he wrote himself in 1914 called *The Spaniard that blighted my life*, a piece good enough to be used by several eminent personalities since with considerable success, and this was followed by *On the good ship Yacki-Hicki-Doola* and *Signora*.

An ambitious man, he had ideas beyond the halls and went into pantomime with great flair and then into revues like 'Hello America' and 'Whirligig'. The audiences still tended to like him best in his old songs and these were generally slipped into the proceedings somewhere. One of his most amusing acrobatic tricks was to hang on to the curtin when it went up to give him a call and to descend again with it. After a fine appearance in 'Rose Marie', he became manager of the Shaftesbury Theatre and put on his own show 'My Son John', which lost him a considerable amount of money. There were many more shows and pantomimes after that but not major successes and it has been suggested that he should have stuck to his natural element the halls. Over-ambitious, perhaps, but always generous with his money, he died in poverty in Charing Cross Hospital.

G. H. Elliott
1884–1962

The 'chocolate-coloured coon' was born in England but first appeared on the stage in America at the age of five. Returning with family to England his first appearance was at Sadler's Wells in 1902. One of his child roles was Little Lord Fauntleroy. By natural selection, he drifted to the Primrose West Minstrels and embarked on his career of coon songs and dancing at the age of nine. Amongst his songs were *I used to sigh for the silvery moon; Hello Susie Green* and *Rastus Brown*. It was a case of sheer charm, agility and smooth art – a great successor to the Eugene Stratton tradition, many of whose songs he included in his act.

Will Fyffe
1885–1947

Will Fyffe, born in Dundee, had a theatrical niché ready made for him. His father, growing tired of life as a shipyard worker, formed a small touring company and Will was soon recruited to play such parts as Little Willy in 'East Lynne' and Little Eva in 'Uncle Tom's Cabin'. In various other companies he continued as a straight actor; meanwhile trying his hand at writing comedy material, none of which he was able to sell. After a long, lean period he got a part in a revue. He finally tried his hand in the provincial halls, and at last was able to use his own material to good purpose. Eventually he got to the Palladium in London – that was in 1921. The following year, there he was in the Royal Command Variety show!

In the old tradition, although the major part of his story lies within the 'variety' era and on the radio, he was a superb character actor and built some wonderful parts for himself – the gamekeeper, the old railway guard, the ship's engineer, a country doctor, a farmer, and so on. But perhaps he is pre-eminently remembered as the very drunken Scotsman who sang *I belong to Glasgow* (*and Glasgow belongs to me*). He first sang the song at the Theatre Royal in Glasgow – it was one of those items he had offered to other Scottish comedians such as Harry Lauder and Neil Kenyon, who had short-sightedly turned it down – and he first used it when asked to deputise for somebody at a moment's notice by the theatre's manager. The band parts had been hastily put together and Will had not really tried out the song on the stage before. It was an immediate hit and landed him lucrative contracts to appear in the Pavilion Theatre, Glasgow for the next three years. Also in town was a London agent who signed him up for the appearance at the London Palladium.

James Agate, later witnessing Will Fyffe's acting of a moving sketch concerning the burying of his friend Jim McGregor, with which he regularly made the theatre stalls damp with tears, was similarly moved and described it as a piece of acting of which 'Garrick could be proud' . . . 'the old actor could not have bettered that mingling of pathos and grotesquerie' . . . 'here is a genius', he wrote.

He could have been a straight actor (he played Hamlet and Richard III in his time); he could have been a film star (he appeared in several with great success); he was a superb mimic with Beerbohm Tree, George Formby Sr., Jack Pleasants and Billy Merson amongst his victims when this was a part of his act in the earlier days. Possibly Will Fyffe knew for a long time that what you needed was simply a good song; he even knew he had one. Eventually *I belong to Glasgow* made its mark and set the direction of his true genius. The real spirit of the music-hall could certainly not have been called dead while Will Fyffe was still around.

I told you your luck lies there.
Good luck.
Will. 1929

Nº 2072.

Jogging Along Behind the Old Grey Mare

(John & Mary)

Fox Trot Song

WITH UKULELE OR "BANJULELE BANJO" ACCOMPANIMENT.

Written and Composed by JOHN P. LONG.

Sung by RANDOLPH SUTTON.

London: FRANCIS, DAY & HUNTER LTD, 138-140, CHARING CROSS ROAD, W.C.2.

NEW YORK AGENTS: LEO FEIST, Inc., 231-5, WEST 40TH STREET.
SYDNEY AGENTS: J. ALBERT & SON, 137-139, KING STREET.
PARIS AGENTS: PUBLICATIONS, FRANCIS-DAY S.A., 30, RUE DE L'ECHIQUIER.
BERLIN AGENTS: FRANCIS, DAY & HUNTER G.m.b.H. LEIPZIGER STR 37. W. 8.

PRINTED IN ENGLAND.

6D NET.

Randolph Sutton
1888–1969

One of the last of the male stars who just came into our 'golden age' prior to the First World War, Randolph Sutton first appeared on the stage in 'Uncle Tom's Cabin' in 1913, and made his London debut at the London Pavilion in 1915. Identified by a classification that would have meant little to the early performers as 'light comedian', he carried on a tradition of saucy and tuneful songs that have much of the old music hall spirit in them: *When are you going to lead me to the altar, Walter; Round the Marble Arch* and his celebrated *On Mother Kelly's doorstep*. If the feel of these songs is clearly of the 1930s, they just as clearly represent the last lingering echoes of the old days that were revived in Don Ross's 'Thanks for the Memory' company, which had many a great old-timer in its ranks, helping to reinstate the music-hall prior to its great present-day revival. He made his last record in January 1969 – *Mother Kelly; Your dog's come home again* and *We're going to the circus* – and died in February. Like all the best stars in our story, Randolph Sutton was full of vitality, filled the stage with a personal charm, and was truly professional in everything he did.

John   and Ma-ry   Jog-ging a - long be-hind the old grey mare.

Clarice Mayne
1891–1966

She has been described by one writer as 'the perfect principal boy' for she was sublime in figure, graceful in deportment, with a glittering smile and an attractive husky voice, every word perfectly heard. But more than that, and what made her one of the great stars of the later halls and variety was, yet again, that knack of finding great songs. She did it in a very practical way by being married to a first-rate composer, James W. Tate (1876-1922). His creations ranged from *Somewhere a voice is calling* to some of the best numbers in 'The Maid of the Mountains' – such as *A bachelor gay* – and many songs which could have risen to the top of the music-hall hit parade at any period in its history – *Every little while; If I should plant a tiny seed of love; A broken doll* and *I was a good little girl*. All of these Clarice Mayne sang with delicious coyness accompanied by Mr. Tate, who was generally referred to as 'That'. He played with great artistry and acted the part of the love-struck husband with honest but silent conviction. At the end of the act, rewarded by a dazzling smile, he would swagger off the stage in a great glow of possessive pride and earn his own round of applause.

There were other great songs that Clarice Mayne put amongst the unforgettables – like *Joshuah* and *Put on your tat-ta little girlie* – and which she continued to sing long after poor old 'That' had died of sheer overwork (his output for pantomimes alone was quite phenomenal). Clarice Mayne later married another fine trouper, Teddie Knox of the Crazy Gang. She remained a most gracious and charming lady until her death in 1966.

Ladies . . .

There are so many fine music-hall artistes not mentioned in this brief volume that we must try to make amends for our discourteous neglect by trying to mention a few that should certainly not be forgotten, particularly those who have been connected with some memorable music-hall ditty.

The inclusion of Vesta Tilley invites inevitable mention and comparison of various rivals and disciples who also excelled in the art of male impersonation. Ella Shields (1879-1952) was a great performer who made this kind of act her speciality from 1910 onwards, and did well to outdo the great Vesta in at least one respect with a song called *I'm Burlington Bertie from Bow* which is probably the one we remember rather than Vesta Tilley's *Burlington Bertie*. Hetty King we can hardly forget. She is still on the stage, as meticulously professional as ever, still smoking the best cigars in her jaunty masher act, puffing that most lethal looking pipe as she does her famous sailor act, and still singing her immortal *All the nice girls love a sailor* – or *Ship ahoy*, as it appears in the publisher's lists. Another song she sang with great success was *I'm afraid to go home in the dark*.

The name of Lottie Collins (1866-1910) will never be forgotten, if only for her frantic performance of that most idiotic but memorable song *Ta-ra-ra-boom-de-ay* which she sung and danced with such abandon and savage gaiety (often three times a night) that she literally exhausted herself to death with it and had a tragically short life. Also to her credit, a famous daughter José Collins, remembered as a star of the musical comedy stage, particularly in 'The Maid of the Mountains'.

A name always mentioned by other stars with respect and affection was that of Bessie Bellwood 1857-1896), a tough, rough and great-hearted woman who also wore herself out at the age of 39 and is remembered for her song *Wot cheer, Ria*. Ella Retford was grace personified, a sparkling personality, a great principal boy, a dainty delight as she sang *Hello there, little Tommy Atkins*.

We cannot mention all the charming ladies of music-hall, but space must be found for a reference to Grace La Rue, who sang the immortal *You made me love you*; Fanny Wentworth, who charmed the sentimental with *The tin gee-gee*; Gertie Gitana, who became a sort of music-hall legend; Katie Lawrence, who could not be missed if only because she sang the song that everyone knows, whether a music-hall enthusiast or not – *Daisy Bell* or *A bicycle made for two*; Lily Burnard with *Two little girls in blue*; Daisy Dormer who sang *I wouldn't leave my little wooden hut for you*; Cissie and Marie Loftus . . . well, even with the best of intentions, many more must be left with a mere gentlemanly acknowledgment of all they did and of the wonderful entertainment they gave.

We will end our praise of the ladies with a tribute to one who is often thought of as the last great star of the halls, although her immense talent went far beyond the bounds of the variety stage, Gracie Fields, now installed as the Duchess of Capri. One has only to mention the titles of songs like *Lead me to the altar, Walter* or *The biggest aspidistra in the world*, and, of course the other kind like *Sally* or *Bless this house* to recall a magnificent voice that can still sing them straight and true or crack up into the most plaintive wheeze that ever crept on to a stage. In a book on the subject of music-hall we could hardly forget 'our Gracie'.

. . . and Gentlemen

Here we might be accused not so much of enforced omission as of downright negligence, having not found a place for a star of the magnitude of Herbert Campbell (1844-1904) for instance. If he is mainly remembered as the foil to Dan Leno in many a Drury Lane pantomime, this great John Bull of a man, weighing nineteen stone, was a master of mirth, parody and satire, to whom nothing was sacred. We will remember him by that artful song, *At my time of life*, which poked fun at 'modern' feminine fashions.

Then there was T. E. Dunville, who died in 1924, who was a pioneer creator of one of those well-intentioned acts where everything goes wrong; and J. C. Heffron, who died in 1934, who would hardly be remembered at all today if he had not introduced an immortal and oft-quoted song to the world – *Where did you get that hat?*

Again, if only for the sake of crediting the songs they sang, we must recall artistes like J. W. Rickaby (1870-1929) who sang *They built Piccadilly for me*; Morny Cash, who died in 1938, who had a wonderful song that has been much revived of late – *I live in Trafalgar Square*. Charles Godfrey (1852-1900) sang *After the ball* and *Hi-tiddly-hi-ti*; while Alec Hurley, who was one of Marie Lloyd's husbands, had an earlier version of *The Lambeth Walk*; Tom Leamore (1866-1939) also sang *They built Piccadilly*, with a great hit of the day in *Percy from Pimlico*; George Beauchamp (1863-1901) will certainly be remembered for his connection with *She was a sweet little dicky-bird* and a song that once provided a very popular catch-phrase – *Get your hair cut*; and Harry Bedford was in the same line of business with *A little bit off the top*. Harry Fragson (1869-1913) was a talented songwriter who wrote songs like *Hullo, who's your lady friend* as well as a very popular entertainer with a French styled act. He was one of many music-hall artistes who had a tragic end, being shot by his own father in a fit of jealousy. We could hardly forget George Bastow (1872-1914) who had a roaring success with that undying ditty, *The galloping major*; Charles Whittle and *Let's all go down the Strand*; Whit Cunliffe with *Who were you with last night* and *Now are we all here*; and George Lashwood, reckoned as one of the last of the lion-comiques, who stirred many hearts with *Goodbye, Dolly Gray* and that sentimental number *In the twi-twi-twilight*. It may have been the singers who made the song in the first place, but they were well rewarded for it, in terms of immortality, by now being remembered for the songs they sang.

We should not overlook some great North country comedians; Jack Pleasants (1875-1924) who sang that delightful ditty *I'm shy, Mary Ellen* and a number that has possibly been sung far too much for its useful sentiments rather than its intrinsic value *I'm twenty-one today*; Jack Smiles also sang *Mary Ellen* and had a hit with a repetitive song called *For months and months and months*; and George Formby Sr., who died of tuberculosis in 1921, had a nice little song called *Standing on the corner of the street*, which his equally great son took on later in his own inimitable style. In fact, we could go on for months and months and months, but mustn't, and can only apologise to those we have neglected. . . .

TAILPIECE

The music-hall would never have 'died' had it not been that the essential spirit that nurtured it died first. The First World War damaged the world spiritually and morally; the Second World War re-opened a partly-healed wound. After these two immeasurable tragedies things could not really be the same. Thereafter pessimism gained an irradicable hold. This is not to say that there is no further ray of hope in the human mind; there is a great deal of humour and love left but the prevailing spirit, as reflected in today's entertainment, is a rather morbid brooding on the sadder and more sordid side of life. The prevailing spirit of music-hall, rightly or wrongly – and many now sincerely mock the brave pretentions of Victorian and Edwardian times that hid a multitude of sins and inequalities – was of optimism. There was no place then for forebodings of despair and disaster. Povery was portrayed, tragedy and the coarser side of life were not glossed over by any means, but the lesson preached in popular entertaniment was that the sturdy human spirit of optimism would always prevail in the end; the sense of humour could always help you to survive. They didn't brood on despair; they pushed it aside and allowed a good song and crude joke to persuade them, for a while, that life was all for the best. We couldn't help the change of spirit that killed music-hall-style entertainment but it is obvious that, in our ever-increasing love for and interest in the 'good old days' (that weren't really good at all) that we still have a strong desire to recover some of its spirit. The more we hear of it, the more chance there will be of some of it being revived.

The music-hall as a thriving entity is dead, but there are still plenty of men and women about who maintain the tradition. Some of the older school like Ted Ray and Arthur Askey are healthy survivors who would have been perfectly at home in the rough and tumble of the halls; so would irresistibly funny men like Morecambe and Wise. They delight us so much because they still persist, against all current trends, in the belief that entertainment is a healthy and beneficial antidote to depression.

That's what music-hall provided in a period when poverty's other antidotes were a good deal less wholesome than even the earthiest of music-hall jokes and songs.

100 Great Music-Hall Songs

TITLE	WRITTEN BY (composer first)	SUNG BY
Act on the square, boys	Alfred Vance	Alfred Vance
After the ball	Charles K. Harris	Vesta Tilley
All the nice girls love a sailor (Ship ahoy)	Bennett Scott; A. J. Mills	Hetty King
Any old iron	Charles Collins; Terry Sheppard	Harry Champion
Archibald, certainly not	Alfred Glover; John L. St. John	George Robey
Are we to part like this	Harry Castling & Mark Collins	Kate Carney
Army of today's all right, The	Kenneth Lyle; Fred W. Leigh	Vesta Tilley
Ask a policeman	A. E. Durandeau; E. W. Rogers	James Fawn
At my time of life	T. W. Connor	Herbert Campbell
At Trinity Church	Fred Gilbert	Tom Costello
Blind boy, The	G. W. Moore; R. Lee	G. H. Chirgwin
Boiled beef and carrots	Charles Collins & Fred Murray	Harry Champion
Boy I love is up in the gallery, The	George Ware	Nellie Power, Marie Lloyd
Broken doll, A	James W. Tate; Clifford Harris	Clarice Mayne
Burlington Bertie from Bow	William Hargreaves	Ella Shields
Captain Jinks of the Horse Marines	Harry Clifton	Harry Rickards
Captain Gingah	Fred W. Leigh	George Bastow
Champagne Charlie	Alfred Lee; George Leybourne	George Leybourne
Comrades	Felix McGlennon	Tom Costello
Daddy wouldn't buy me a bow-wow	Joseph Tabrar	Vesta Victoria
Daisy Bell	Harry Dacre	Katie Lawrence
Dear old pals	G. W. Hunt	G. H. MacDermott
Don't dilly dally on the way	Charles Collins & Fred W. Leigh	Marie Lloyd
Down at the old Bull and Bush	Harry von Tilzer; Andrew B. Sterling	Florrie Forde
Down the road	Fred Gilbert	Gus Elen
Every little while	James W. Tate; Clifford Harris	Lee White, Clarice Mayne
Flanagan	C. W. Murphy and Will Letters	Florrie Forde
Following in father's footsteps	E. W. Rogers	Vesta Tilley
For old time's sake	Charles Osborne	Millie Lindon
Future Mrs. 'Awkins, The	Albert Chevalier	Albert Chevalier
Galloping Major, The	George Bastow & Fred W. Leigh	George Bastow
Goodbye, Dolly Gray	Paul Barnes; Will D. Cobb	George Lashwood
Has anybody here seen Kelly	C. W. Murphy & Will Letters	Florrie Forde
Has anybody seen my tiddler	A. J. Mills & Frank W. Carter	Millie Payne
Hello, hello, who's your lady friend	Harry Fragson; Worton David & Bert Lee	Mark Sheridan
Here we are, here we are, here we are again	Charles Knight & Kenneth Lyle	Mark Sheridan
Hold your hand out, naughty boy	C. W. Murphy & Worton David	Florrie Forde
Honeysuckle and the bee, The	William H. Penn; Albert H. Fitz	Ellaline Terriss

I belong to Glasgow	Will Fyffe	Will Fyffe
I do like to be beside the seaside	John A. Glover-Kind	Mark Sheridan
I live in Trafalgar Square	C. W. Murphy	Morny Cash
I love a lassie	Harry Lauder & Gerald Grafton	Harry Lauder
I may be crazy	Leslie Stuart	Eugene Stratton
I used to sigh for the silvery moon	Hermann Darewski; Lester Barrett	G. H. Elliott
I was a good little girl	James W. Tate; Clifford Harris	Clarice Mayne
If it wasn't for the 'ouses in between	George Le Brunn; Edgar Bateman	Gus Elen
If those iips could only speak	Charles Ridgewell; Will Godwin	Will Godwin
I'm Henery the Eighth	Fred Murray & Bert Weston	Harry Champion
I'm shy, Mary Ellen	George A. Stevens & Charles Ridgewell	Jack Pleasants
In the twi-twi-twilight	Hermann Darewski; Charles Wilmot	George Lashwood
It's a bit of a ruin that Cromwell knocked about a bit	Harry Bedford; Terry Sullivan	Marie Lloyd
It's a great big shame	George Le Brunn; Edgar Bateman	Gus Elen
It's all right in the summertime	Fred Murray & George Everard	Vesta Victoria
It's a long way to Tipperary	Jack Judge & Harry Williams	Florrie Forde
Joshuah	George Arthurs & Bert Lee	Clarice Mayne
Just like the ivy	Harry Castling; A. J. Mills	Marie Kendall
Keep right on to the end of the road	Harry Lauder	Harry Lauder
Knocked 'em in the old Kent Road (Wot cher)	Charles Ingle & Albert Chevalier	Albert Chevalier
Let's all go down the Strand	Harry Castling & C. W. Murphy	Charles R. Whittle
Lily of Laguna, The	Leslie Stuart	Eugene Stratton
Limerick Races	Traditional	Sam Collins
Little Dolly Daydream	Leslie Stuart	Eugene Stratton
Little of what you fancy, A	Fred W. Leigh & George Arthurs	Marie Lloyd
Man on the flying trapeze, The	Alfred Lee; George Leybourne	George Leybourne
Man who broke the bank at Monte Carlo, The	Fred Gilbert	Charles Coborn
Married to a mermaid	Arthur Lloyd	Arthur Lloyd
Miner's dream of home, The	Will Godwin & Leo Dryden	Leo Dryden
My fiddle is my sweetheart	G. H. Chirgwin; Harry Hunter	G. H. Chirgwin
My old Dutch	Charles Ingle; Albert Chevalier	Albert Chevalier
Now I have to call him Father	Charles Collins & Fred Godfrey	Vesta Victoria
Not for Joseph	Alfred Lee & F. W. Green	Arthur Lloyd
Oh, oh, Antonio	C. W. Murphy & Dan Lipton	Florrie Forde
Oh, Mr. Porter	George Le Brunn; Thomas Le Brunn	Marie Lloyd
On the good ship 'Yacki-hicki-doo-la'	Billy Merson	Billy Merson
Our lodger's such a nice young man	Fred Murray & Laurence Barclay	Vesta Victoria
Pack up your troubles	Felix Powell & George Asaf	Florrie Forde
Poor John	Henry E. Pether; Fred W. Leigh	Vesta Victoria
Pretty Polly Perkins	Traditional; Harry Clifton	Harry Clifton
Put me up on an island	Will Letters	Wilkie Bard
Put on your tat-ta little girlie	Fred W. Leigh	Clarice Mayne
Rat-catcher's daughter, The	Traditional	Sam Cowell
Roamin' in the gloamin'	Harry Lauder	Harry Lauder
Sam Hall	Traditional	W. G. Ross

Song	Author(s)	Performer
She sells seashells	Harry Gifford; Terry Sullivan	Wilkie Bard
She was one of the early birds	T. W. Connor	George Beauchamp
Shelling green peas	Harry Clifton	Harry Clifton
Ship I love, The	Felix McGlennon	Tom Costello
Spaniard that blighted my life, The	Billy Merson	Billy Merson
Swing me higher, Obadiah	Maurice Scott; Alf E. Rick	Florrie Forde
Ta-ra-ra-boom-de-ay	Henry J. Sayers	Lottie Collins
Tommy make room for your uncle	T. S. Lonsdale	W. B. Fair
Two lovely black eyes	Charles Coborn	Charles Coborn
Up in a balloon boys	G. W. Hunt; George Leybourne	George Leybourne
Vilikins and his Dinah	Traditional	Sam Cowell
Waiting at the Church	Henry E. Pether; Fred W. Leigh	Vesta Victoria
We don't want to fight	G. W. Hunt	G. H. McDermott
What's that for, eh!	George Le Brunn; W. T. Lytton	Marie Lloyd
When father papered the parlour	Weston & Barnes	Billy Williams
Where did you get that hat	James Rolmaz	J. C. Heffron
Who were you with last night	Fred Godfrey & Mark Sheridan	Mark Sheridan

Bibliography

1. Basic books of reference

THE VARIETY STAGE by Charles Douglas Stuart and A. J. Park (T. Fisher Unwin) 1895. The first treatise on music-hall written during its early and flourishing years. Still possibly the most fascinating account, invaluable for its contemporary information on the halls and the incidental characters. A rare volume.

SIXTY YEARS' STAGE SERVICE (Life of Charles Morton) by W. H. Morton and H. Chance Newton (Gale & Polden) 1905. Important biography of the 'Father of the Halls', the Canterbury, the Oxford and valuable incidental information. Also scarce.

IDOLS OF THE HALLS by H. Chance Newton (Heath Cranton) 1928. Intimate memories, eye-witness portraits but hazy on facts.

THE STORY OF THE MUSIC HALL by Archibald Haddon (Fleetway) 1935. Honest but superficial account.

WINKLES AND CHAMPAGNE by M. Willson Disher (Batsford) 1938. A beautifully produced book which, though not entirely devoted to music-hall, is worthwhile for its fine illustrations (many in colour) and its sensible comments.

STARS WHO MADE THE HALLS by S. Theodore Felstead (T. Werner Laurie) 1946. Useful book of first-hand impressions of many music-hall stars.

THE EARLY DOORS by Harold Scott (Nicholson & Watson) 1946. First scholarly account of music-hall history. A well written book which will eventually be recognised as a classic. The same author's collection AN ENGLISH SONG BOOK is a valuable source of 17th/19th century popular musical material (Chapman & Hall) 1925.

THE MELODIES LINGER ON by W. Macqueen-Pope (W. H. Allen) 1951. A bulky history written in the author's usual emotional style; a lot of knowledge which would have been more valuable if more accurate and specific.

THEY WERE SINGING by Christopher Pulling (Harrap) 1952. A penetrating work on the actual music and its relation to the social background. But sadly lacking in dates, as usual in this sphere.

BRITISH MUSIC HALL by Raymond Mander and Joe Mitchenson (Studio Vista) 1965. An impressive book by the two famous archivists, packed full of splendid pictures and material from their collection. A considerable amount of information in extended captions and a typical introductory account from starry-eyed John Betjeman.

SWEET SATURDAY NIGHT by Colin MacInnes (MacGibbon & Kee) 1967; (Panther) 1969. Discursive, nostalgic and interesting comments.

THE NORTHERN MUSIC HALL by G. J. Mellor (Graham) 1970. Emphasis on halls outside London but also gives a thorough and interesting account of music hall in general.

2. *Autobiographies and biographies*

ALBERT CHEVALIER: A RECORD BY HIMSELF by Albert Chevalier and Brian Daly (Macqueen) 1896.

BEFORE I FORGET by Albert Chevalier (Fisher Unwin) 1901.

LIFE AND REMINISCENCES by G. H. Chirgwin (Bennett), 1912.

THE MAN WHO BROKE THE BANK by Charles Coborn (Hutchinson) n.d.

THE COWELLS IN AMERICA (Sam Cowell) ed. M. Willson Disher (Oxford) 1934.

THE AUTOBIOGRAPHY OF AN ECCENTRIC COMEDIAN by T. E. Dunville (Everett) n.d.

A MODERN COLUMBUS by R. G. Knowles (Laurie) 1918.

AT HOME AND ON TOUR by Harry Lauder (Greening) 1912; A MINSTREL IN FRANCE by, Harry Lauder (Melrose) 1918; ROAMIN' IN THE GLOAMIN' by Harry Lauder (Hutchinson) 1927.

HYS BOOKE: A VOLUME OF FRIVOLITIES by Dan Leno (Greening) 1901; Abridged reprint (ed. Roy Hudd) 1968.

DAN LENO by J. Hickory Wood (Methuen) 1905.

OUR MARIE (Marie Lloyd) by Naomi Jacob (Hutchinson) 1936.

MARIE LLOYD, QUEEN OF THE MUSIC-HALLS by W. Macqueen-Pope (Oldbourne) n.d.

FIXING THE STOOF OOP by Billy Merson (Hutchinson) n.d.

STORIES AND ANECDOTES by 'Jolly' John Nash n.d.; THE MERRIEST MAN ALIVE by 'Jolly' John Nash, n.d.

HARRY RANDALL, OLD TIME COMEDIAN by Harry Randall (Low) n.d.

TAKE IT FOR A FACT by Ada Reeve (Heinemann) 1954.

A BOOK OF TRAVELS (AND WANDERINGS) by Harry Relph (Little Tich) (Greening) 1911.

FIFTY YEARS OF SPOOF by Arthur Roberts (Lane) 1927.

MY LIFE UP TO NOW by George Robey (Greening) 1908; LOOKING BACK ON LIFE by George Robey (Constable) 1933.

PRIME MINISTER OF MIRTH (George Robey) by A. E. Wilson (Odhams) 1956.

RECOLLECTIONS OF VESTA TILLEY by Lady de Frece (Vesta Tilley) (Hutchinson) 1934.

REMINISCENCES OF J. L. TOOLE by Joseph Hatton (Hurst & Blackett) 1889.

3. *Other books with sections, chapters or essays on aspects of music-hall*

IMMOMENT TOYS (1945) by James Agate

MR. PUNCH'S MODEL MUSIC-HALL SONGS AND DRAMAS (1892) by F. Anstey.

BOW BELL MEMORIES (n.d.) by Louis Bamberger.

MORE (1899); MAINLY ON THE AIR (1946); AROUND THEATRES (1953); MORE THEATRES (1969); LAST THEATRES (1970) by Sir Max Beerbohm.

OLD PINK 'UN DAYS (1924); LONDON TOWN (1929); PINK PARADE (1933); A PINK 'UN REMEMBERS (1937); THE DAYS WE KNEW (1943); SEVENTY YEARS OF SONG (editor) (1943) by J. B. Booth.

LONDON IN MY TIME (1934) by Thomas Burke.

'THE PERFORMER' WHO'S WHO IN VARIETY (1950) by G. R. Bullar and L. Evans.

FULL SCORE (1970) by Sir Neville Cardus.

MUSIC HALL NIGHTS (1925) by Dion Clayton Calthrop (not a factual book).

CROWDED NIGHTS AND DAYS (1930) by Arthur Croxton.

SELECTED ESSAYS 1917-1932 (1932) by T. S. Eliot.

OLD-TIME MUSIC HALL COMEDIANS (1949) by Sir Louis Fergusson.

MY MELODIOUS MEMORIES (1937) by Herman Finck.

MUSIC-HALL LAND (1900) by Percy Fitzgerald.

THE 'HALLS' (n.d.) by George Gamble. Illustrations by G. F. Scotson-Clark.

JIMMY GLOVER–HIS BOOK (1911); JIMMY GLOVER AND HIS FRIENDS (1913); HIMS ANCIENT AND MODERN (1926) by Jimmy Glover.

FIFTY YEARS OF A LONDONER'S LIFE (1916); A PLAYGOER'S MEMORIES (1920) by H. G. Hibbert.

MUSIC OF THE PEOPLE (1970) by Edward Lee.

MUSIC HALL STARS OF THE NINETIES (1952) by George Le Roy.

POPULAR ENTERTAINMENT THROUGH THE AGES (1932) by Samuel McKechnie.

SEVEN CENTURIES OF POPULAR SONG (1956) by Reginald Nettel.

WHO'S WHO IN THE THEATRE (1916) ed. John Parker. Special music-hall supplement.

LATE JOYS AT THE PLAYER'S THEATRE (1943) ed. Jean Anderson.

The London Music Hall Artiste's Vade Mecum or Constant Companion (1899) by Brandon Phillips.

Music-Hall Memories (1927) ed. Terence Prentis.

Swings and Roundabouts (1919) by T. McDonald Rendle.

Minstrel Memories (1928) by Harry Reynolds.

Ring Up the Curtain (1938) by Ernest Short & Arthur Compton-Rickett.

Fifty Years of Vaudeville (1946) by Ernest Short.

Players' Joys (1962) by Hal. D. Stewart.

Old Music Halls (1900) by Sir Richard Terry.

From Theatre to Music Hall (1912) by W. R. Titterton.

London in the Sixties (1909) by One of the Old Brigade.

Victorian Song: From Dive to Drawing Room (1955) by M. Willson Disher.

Fairs, Circuses and Music-Halls (1942) by M. Willson Disher.

DISCOGRAPHY OF LPs

1. *Original recordings re-issued*

Top of the Bill – items by Lauder (2), Little Tich, Lloyd (2), Stratton (2), Forde (2), Chevalier (2), Leno – Fidelio ATL4010.

The Golden Age of the Music Hall – items by Elen, Victoria, Chevalier (2), Lloyd (2), Leno (2), Bradfield, Robey, Roberts, Lytton, Little Tich, Forde – Delta TQD3030.

Golden Voices of the Music Hall – items by Shields (2), Leamore (2), Wallace (2), Elen (2), King (2), Whelan (2) – Decca ACL1077.

Stars Who Made the Music Hall – Sutton, Carney, Elen, King, Pleasants, Forde, Coborn, Jackley, Morris, Formby, Bennett, Merson, O'Shea, Russell – Decca ACL1170.

The Great Days of Music Hall – items by (selections) Merson, Victoria, Coborn, Forde, Champion, Retford – Music for Pleasure MFP1146.

On Mother Kelly's Doorstep – items by Randolph Sutton – Decca ACL1266.

Music-Hall to Variety, 1-3 – items by Chevalier, Mayne, Bastow, Robey, Stratton, Forde, Whelan, Formby Sr., Williams, Champion, Shields, Elliott, Lloyd, Emney, Reeve, Fragson, Tate, Morris, Flotsam & Jetsam, Layton & Johnstone, Hay, Sarony, Penrose, Tucker, Bennett, Clare, Kenney, Fields, O'Shea, Frankau, Crazy Gang, Wallace, Holloway, Waters, Miller, Desmond, Western Bros., Wilton, etc. – 3 Vols. World Record Club SH148/9/50.

The World of Music Hall – items by Sarony, Forde, Danvers, Robey, Kendall, Whelan, Comber, Miller, Lloyd Jr., Tubb – Decca PA81.

Harry Lauder, Esq. of Laudervale – items by Lauder – Transatlantic XTRA1097.

Sir Harry Lauder – items by Lauder – Ember EMB3404.

2. *New recordings of Music Hall material*

The Birth of the Music Hall – World Record Club T797, (S) ST 797.

Champagne Charlie – Stanley Holloway – WRC T325, (S) ST325.

Join in the Chorus – Stanley Holloway – WRC T912, (S) ST912.

Leonard Sachs–Old Time Music Hall – WRC T667, (S) ST667.

The Good Old Days – Leonard Sachs – CBS (S) 63077.

Mister Benjamin Hawthorne's Original Olde Tyme Music Hall – Saga (S) SOC1042.

Heart-Rending Ballads and Raucous Ditties – Julie Andrews – CBS (S) SBPG62405.

The 'Ouses in Between – John Foreman – Reality RY1004.

An Evening at Vauxhall Gardens in 1851 – Rare Recorded Editions RRE100.

Your Own, Your Very Own – in preparation.

Inclusion of a record in these lists is no indication of its present availability.